QB
65
.W54
1995

The Mapping of the Heavens

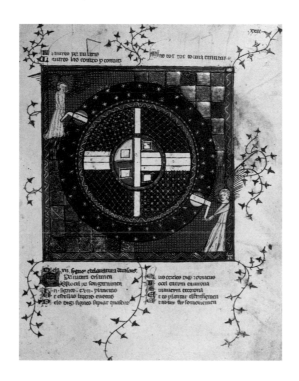

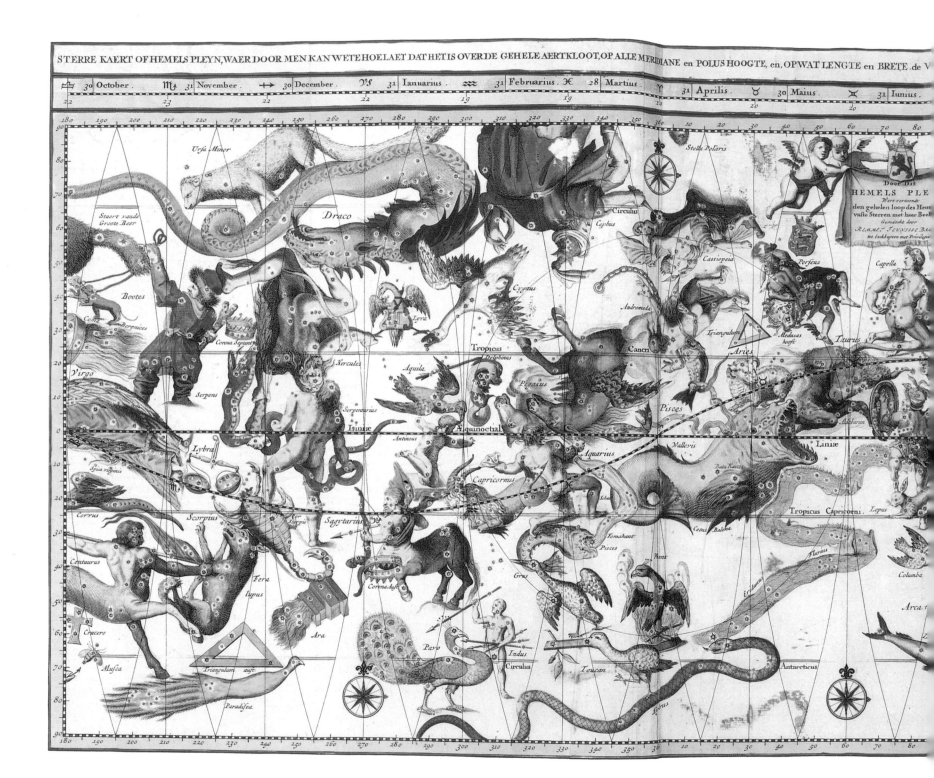

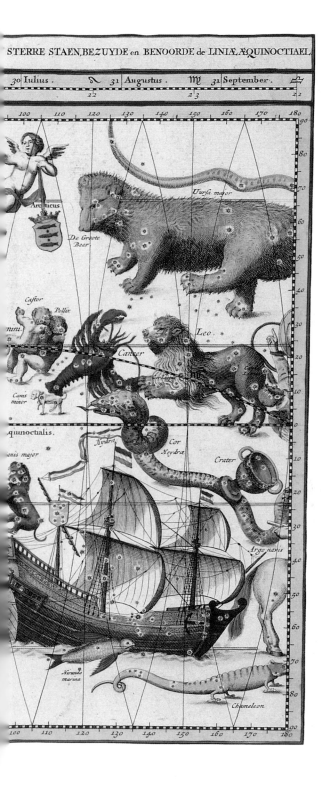

The Mapping
of the Heavens

PETER WHITFIELD

Pomegranate Artbooks • San Francisco
in association with The British Library

Front and rear endpapers: from F. Argelander, *Uranometria Nova*, 1843. The British Library 14000.c.42

Half-title: Angels Turning the cosmic mechanism, from a fifteenth-century manuscript. The British Library, Harley MS 4940, f.28

Title page: Backer's Star Chart, *c.*1710. The Library of Congress, Washington D.C.

First published 1995 by The British Library
Published in North and South America by
Pomegranate Artbooks, Box 6099,
Rohnert Park, California 94927

ISBN 0–87654–475–8
Pomegranate Catalog No. A803

Designed by John Mitchell
Typeset by Bexhill Phototypesetters, Bexhill-on-Sea, East Sussex
Printed in Singapore by Craft Print

Contents

'The strongest affection and utmost zeal should, I think, promote the studies concerned with the most beautiful objects. This is the discipline which deals with the universe's divine revolutions, the stars' motions, sizes, distances, risings and settings . . . for what is more beautiful than heaven? By virtue of heaven's transcendent perfection, most philosophers have called it a visible god . . . .
However this divine rather than human science is not free from perplexities . . .'

– Copernicus:
On the Revolutions of the Heavenly Spheres,
1543

Fig. N.

Colurus Æquinoctiorum.

Andromeda.

Perseus.

Jacea.

CASSIOPEIA.

Camelopardalus.

Latitudo.

Longitudo.

Preface

THIS BOOK TRACES THE HISTORY OF ASTRONOMY through its images, in particular through the development of celestial maps, where science and art came together in the attempt to shape a rational image of the heavens.

To watch and interpret the skies has always been one of man's fundamental instincts. In all pre-industrial societies, real darkness filled a great part of men's lives, and ancient civilizations built up a knowledge of the skies that was more precise than their knowledge of the world in which they lived. To impose order on the expanse of star-filled sky, star groups in the form of animals, gods and heroes were created to be landmarks in the sky. With the heavens mapped in this way, its patterns could be used as fundamental gauges of direction and, most importantly, of time, for no civilization could progress without a calendar.

But alongside this precise, observed regularity there was always the mystery of the skies: not content merely to observe, astronomers sought to explain the causes of what they saw. All civilizations have invested the heavens with transcendent powers, while some have claimed to discover in the stars laws governing man's mind and body, his origin and his future. For many thousands of years, in many different cultures, divination was an essential part of astronomy. Hence astronomy was intimately related to religion, both pagan and Christian, and the study of the mechanism of the universe became also a search for the creator and ruler of it.

Celestial maps as we know them emerged during the Renaissance and flourished throughout the age of science. They were a product of the Renaissance sense of ordered space, the sense which also saw the development of perspective, terrestrial mapping and scientific diagrams. As they sought ever-greater precision and fullness, the mapmakers of the age of science became engaged in a process of demystification of the heavens. At the same time these maps became a minor art-form, and were overlaid with elaborate constellation imagery, both classical and contemporary. In the nineteenth century, astro-photography began to revolutionize celestial mapping, and deep-space photography now provides much of the fundamental data of modern cosmology. These images from the edge of infinity have had the effect of awakening a new mysticism within the austerities of secular science.

This is not a technical book but I hope that astronomers may still read it with some pleasure. Of all the sciences, the history of astronomy is the most resonant with a sense of mystery and intellectual excitement: I believe that maps and other images of the heavens succeed in some degree in conveying that resonance.

I am grateful to a distinguished historian of astronomy, Professor John North, for commenting on this text and making many valuable suggestions; but he does not

HEVELIUS: CASSIOPEIA from *Uranographia*, 1690.
The British Library, 532.k.19

necessarily subscribe to the ideas which I put forward here. The Royal Astronomical Society, through their librarian Peter Hingley, generously allowed me to use their excellent library for research. The Bodleian Library and the British Library proved themselves, as always, to be priceless links with the past.

Peter Whitfield
February 1995

Introduction

STAR CHARTS AND CLASSICAL ASTRONOMY

IN THE PAGES THAT FOLLOW some of the images with which astronomers and artists have represented the pattern of the stars in the sky will be described and illustrated. But the way people have seen the heavenly sphere is inseparable from the way they have thought about it, and the subject of heaven is undeniably a large one. The material of astronomy — the heavens — has always been seen to have a spiritual dimension as well as a physical reality. We are dealing with evolving science, but also with its interpretation, its images, and these visual interpretations can rarely be divorced from the way artists have visualized others elements of their world. This means that a history of star maps must be rooted in the history of astronomy, and must be aware of many wider forces at work in the development of human thought. This may sound self-evident, but books have been written about star maps that make almost no reference to their context in astronomy or in wider intellectual history, as though they somehow existed in isolation. In fact throughout most of history the study of astronomy has been inseparably linked with philosophy and religion. Indeed in astrology it produced its own form of pseudo-religion.

By contrast, the core period in the history of published celestial mapping — *c.*1550–1850 — coincides exactly with the mature period of terrestrial mapping, and it acquired an identity of its own; star charts as scientific reference documents, but decorated in the taste of the time, were published, copied, refined and elaborated as a minor art form. The mapping of that period saw the emergence of a consciously scientific approach to cartography through the use of co-ordinates and scales, and progressed to the first exact national topographic surveys. The celestial maps of this period share that cartographic language, handling the techniques of projection, co-ordinates and symbols in order to translate information and concepts into graphic form. There is an interesting circularity in this process: techniques such as co-ordinates and projections had formed an important part of mature Greek science, and they had first been developed with reference to the celestial sphere. After a long period of eclipse during the middle ages, the Renaissance rediscovery of Ptolemy's geography led to the transfer of those techniques from the mapping of the world back to that of the heavens.

Yet of course there were outstanding differences between maps of the heavens and those of the earth. The terrestrial mapmaker was using mathematical skills, theoretical and practical, to represent the world, or part of the world, in a way that he could never see: it was conceptual rather than pictorial. No man could see England or Italy or Africa, yet the mapmaker had to draw them, and also to represent on them a wide range of topographic features. The goal of the celestial mapmaker was much less challenging: to record the relative positions of the stars as he saw them, for there is no topography in

PTOLEMY and the celestial sphere from Regiomontanus *Epytoma in Almagestum Ptolemi*, Venice 1496.
The British Library, IB 23380

the sky requiring symbolic representation. This apparently simple task has led some historians to advocate excluding celestial charts altogether from the history of cartography, and to argue that they are pictures, not essentially different from the pictures which ancient or modern observers might draw of mountains, trees or animals. It is argued that no theoretical or conceptual framework is embodied in a diagram of the stars, as it must be in a terrestrial map.

But this is a reductive argument that fails to do justice to the mature star chart. The Babylonian hunting scene showing the seven stars of the Pleiades may be no more than a picture. But ancient peoples also drew pictures of hills, rivers, horses and kings, and when these elements were displayed as symbols and spatially related, the first maps began to emerge. The primitive star-picture is a vast distance away from the mature star chart as it had evolved by the sixteenth century. The essential thing to grasp about the double-hemisphere star map is that it is not a picture of what is seen in the sky: it is a conceptual model deliberately plotted in order to display the entire heavens. The point of view is an abstract, imaginary point above the north celestial pole, looking down upon the starry sphere. The stars are consciously spread outwards from the pole in a projection, which transfers the spherical surface to two dimensions. This model was derived from Greek geometry and was undoubtedly influenced by a knowledge of Islamic celestial globes and astrolabes. Of course the actual material of the star chart — several hundred points to represent the stars — presented no great difficulty to the mapmaker, and was incapable of any great development. But as a conceptual model requiring a mathematical basis and a visual language, the sixteenth-century star chart shows a direct application of cartographic technique. There was another type of celestial 'map' which has been arguably more important historically than the star chart, namely the cosmic model or diagram, in which the relationships between the earth, sun, planets and stars are visualized. This form of conceptual modelling cannot be said to be cartographic in the strict sense, but the understanding of these relationships has always been fundamental to astronomy and to religion, and cosmic modelling has had a more dynamic history than stellar mapping.

There is however an obvious level on which the star chart parallels terrestrial mapping, namely its use of graphic forms and artistic motifs drawn from contemporary models. The hallmark of the star chart from 1500–1800 is the procession of constellation figures, which invariably attracts the eye and dominates the map. Terrestrial maps of this period are likewise instantly recognizable for their engravings of gods and goddesses, ships and sea-serpents, kings and allegorical figures. Yet no group of maps is as exclusively identified with any image as the star chart is with the constellation-figures. The classical constellations were the creations of the cultures of the ancient near east. The exact origin of most of them is purely conjectural, although it seems probably that they were connected with myths of creation, fertility and the seasons. The origin of even the Greek constellations such as Perseus, whose legends are found in classical writers, cannot be fixed in time, and have parallels in other cultures. The sources of the constellation myths have greatly exercized many writers, but they are of no strictly astronomical importance. The fact that the constellations were adopted across cultures, the Babylonian Zodiac re-appearing in Egypt and Greece for example, argues that their cultic or mythic element was secondary. Their great purpose was mnemonic: to define patterns and 'landmarks' in the sky, with which to measure time and direction. The precise resemblance of a group of a dozen stars to a Bear, a Lion or a Hunter was unimportant; it was the pattern that was vital, and the pattern could best be fixed by imposing on the stars certain well-known cultic images. Adopted by the Egyptians, the Greeks and the Arabs, these mnemonic images survived and flourished again in Renaissance Europe as essential features in the structure of the star chart. It was astrology

of course which played the major role in reinforcing these images, and centuries of such use made them permanent. But they became in time totally detached from any scientific or cultic basis, and served as purely conventional means to locate any region of the sky. For the astronomer, stars were catalogued as the first, second or third star in Scorpio or Leo and so on, in the manner made standard by Ptolemy, while the artistic elaboration of the figures proceeded under its own impetus. The celestial maps of the seventeenth and eighteenth centuries were published almost exclusively for an educated but non-scientific market, who saw them as part of their civilized library, along with their world maps, their architectural engravings, their botanical folios and their Latin classics.

This classical connection is vitally significant. Long after the decline of astrology, the constellations were seen by publishers and readers as a series of classical motifs that could be reproduced and elaborated at will. Just as the architect designed classical facades, the engraver illustrated Plutarch's *Lives*, and the poet laboured over his translation of Virgil, so the map publisher perpetuated the forms of the constellations as a conscious link with the classical past. The mythological associations served to add further resonance to the images. It is almost certain that these twin-hemisphere charts were not used by practising astronomers, except as models to demonstrate the general arrangement of the stars; as observational instruments they were of no more use than a map of the world would be to a mariner navigating the Pacific Ocean. The serious astronomer would use the star catalogue from which the map had been drawn. The great celestial atlases were another matter; the works of Bayer, Hevelius, Flamsteed and Bode were each based on new sky surveys and star catalogues which in their time set new standards of accuracy and fullness. These atlases were composed of a series of detailed charts centred on each constellation, and they may be regarded as the equivalent of the detailed regional maps in a terrestrial atlas.

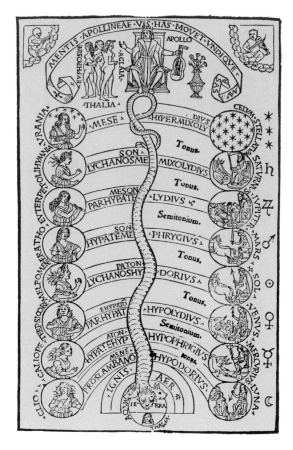

THE MUSIC OF THE SPHERES from Gafori's *Practica Musice*, 1496. Apollo conducts the music of the spheres, each planet ruled by one of the muses, separated by a regular musical interval, and producing one of the classical musical modes. The doctrine of correspondences obsessed the medieval mind: things living and inanimate, earthly and heavenly, physical and spiritual, were all held to be associated in the chain of being.
The British Library, m.k.1.g.3

Both before and after this core period, the pictorial chart of the heavens did not exist, although many other forms of astronomical image did. In the earlier phase the dominant theme is the religious framework within which astronomy and all science was conducted. In the modern age a new generation of photographic star maps and images has developed which have reached out beyond the visible sky and formed the basis of a new cosmology. This study concentrates on European astronomy which has developed continuously down to the present day. In the past, non-European traditions achieved levels of skill in astronomy that were in advance of European practice, but they invariably reached a point where they ceased to develop; there was no Copernican revolution or scientific revolution outside Europe.

In one sense astronomy is science at its most austere: the desire to observe, chart and understand a realm of the universe that was permanently beyond the reach of direct experience, was driven by intellectual curiosity in its purest form. Yet there was a practical and universal motive behind the early study of the heavens, namely to measure time. All civilizations perceived the cyclical pattern in the night sky, and seized upon it as a means of measuring and anticipating the passage of the hours, days, seasons and years. And beneath this technical function lay the religious dimension which all cultures saw in astronomy, and which gave a spiritual urgency to the astronomical quest: the study of the mechanism of the universe became also the search for the creator and sustainer of it. In one of the most famous metaphors in classical literature, Plato compares man's limited perception of reality to that of prisoners chained in a cave:

> The visible realm corresponds to the prison, and the light of the fire in the prison to the power of the sun . . . the ascent into the upper world and the sight of the objects there, represent the upward progress of the mind into the intelligible realm.

Plato, *Republic*, Book 7

Plato's fable of the cave is an apt metaphor for man's early attempts to understand what he saw in the sky. Although not so confined in vision as the cave-prisoners, the ancient observer witnessed an apparent procession of shapes and movements in the heavens, whose true interpretation defied him. The crucial fact — that the apparent movements of the heavenly bodies are largely imparted by man's shifting viewpoint — was not grasped until the sixteenth century. Cosmic models before Copernicus naturally assumed an unmoving earth at the centre of the universe.

The number of stars 'visible to the naked eye' is of course debatable: the maximum figure is perhaps 15,000 (in the whole sky, not all visible together). But even a practised observer can readily identify only a few dozen individual bright stars, and all others must be found by reference first to their brighter neighbours and to the star groups within which they lie. Hence the designation of constellations was a referencing system which all cultures have found essential. The greatest star catalogue of antiquity, that of Claudius Ptolemy *c*.150AD, located slightly more than 1,000 individual stars, and this remained the canonical number until the eighteenth century, when the southern stars were charted and when Flamsteed catalogued some 3,000 stars of the northern sky. Until the invention of the telescope in the early seventeenth century enabled fainter stars and other objects to be seen, the material of astronomy — the face of the heavens — remained what it had been for first 3,000 years of astronomical history.

To any observer, ancient or modern, the sky appears as a dome resting on the surrounding horizon. In the course of each night the stars, fixed in an unchanging pattern

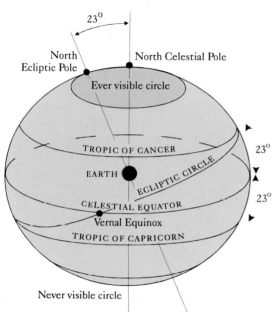

23°

North
Ecliptic Pole · North Celestial Pole

Ever visible circle

TROPIC OF CANCER — 23°

EARTH — *ECLIPTIC CIRCLE*

CELESTIAL EQUATOR — 23°

Vernal Equinox

TROPIC OF CAPRICORN

Never visible circle

STRUCTURE OF THE CELESTIAL SPHERE as analysed by Greek mathematicians. This concept, with the earth at its centre, underlies all classical celestial measurement and mapping.

in relation to each other, appear to move *en masse* across the sky. The movement is not linear, but appears to rotate about a fixed point above one of the earth's poles. To an observer in the northern hemisphere, part of the sky around the north pole is visible throughout this rotation, another section around the south pole is always invisible, while the rest of the sky appears to rise and set each night. The size of these ever-visible and ever-invisible spheres will vary with changing latitude; only on the equator will the entire sky be displayed. Ancient cultures conceived the stars to be set in a starry sphere, and it was this sphere which revolved around the earth. The concept of the starry sphere is still a highly practical one for the observer and the mapmaker.

In addition to this daily revolution, the starry sphere was apparently also shifting in a second and much slower cycle. Stars visible at midnight moved one degree westward each succeeding midnight. New stars appeared on the eastern horizon each nightfall, while in the west other stars vanished and were no longer seen after sunset. In 180 days the rotating sphere of stars changed its aspect completely. Astronomers in some cultures appreciated that this cycle was related to the sun's movement: that the stars were still present in the daytime, but were lost in the stronger light of the sun. Stars visible at midnight will be hidden by the noonday sun 180 days later, so that, for example, the sun is said to be 'in Aries' when the stars of Aries are invisible in May. We would now, express this as a function of the earth's revolution around the sun, but the effect is the same.

An older and quite universal discovery was that five stars were not fixed like the others, but moved independently across the starry sphere. These planets (from the Greek word meaning wanderer) moved in the most puzzling way, each appearing for some period of time to slow down and then reverse its direction through the stars before moving forward once more. The sun-centred orbits of the five planets (Uranus, Neptune and Pluto were of course undiscovered) now serve to explain these motions, as the planets overtake or are overtaken by the earth. But it was this planetary behaviour which caused the greatest difficulties to all early planetary theorists. Like the stars, the sun, moon and planets appeared to revolve independently about the earth in their daily motion, but in addition, over the course of a year, their paths appeared to rise and fall, within certain limits, against the background of the fixed stars. To explain this, the spheres bearing the moon and planets were conceived by Hellenic theorists to bear secondary cycles — epicycles — to explain this dual motion. The fixing of their paths against the starry sphere, the precise modelling of the supposed epicycles, became one of the principal tasks of classical astronomy. The charting of the yearly cycle of the stars, and of the more complex paths of the planets, was not dependent on the modern knowledge that the earth revolves around the sun.

The sun's apparent path through the stars in the course of the year was an important discovery, but it is perhaps not immediately obvious why, since the sun and stars are never visible together. The answer is that this path, called the ecliptic, is a line that is fixed in the sky, and it became the baseline for a locational framework in the heavens. The horizon is of course always shifting, but the ecliptic is an objective reality, which in the context of Greek geometry became the basis for a mature referencing system. The extremes of the ecliptic, the highest and lowest points touched by the sun, the tropics, were also seen to coincide closely with the region of the sky within which the moon and planets reached their extreme positions, and this part of the sky attracted the greatest attention. As the geometry of eclipses came to be understood, it was seen that they occurred only in this zone, hence its name. When moonlight was recognized to be reflected sunlight, it was understood that the full moon was directly opposite the sun, while the new moon was hidden against the sun. We now know that the sun's apparent rise and fall along the ecliptic are caused by the earth itself, whose axis is tilted at roughly

5

THE CONSTELLATION AURIGA from Bode's
atlas *Uranographia*, 1801.

23 degrees from the perpendicular. As the earth slowly circles the sun, the observer will
see the sun apparently rise and fall and rise again in an annual cycle. Age-old myths such
as that of Persephone and Hades expressed an intuitive perception of the cyclic pattern
in time and nature; but well before the fifth century BC it was understood, on a scientific
level, that this rise and fall of the sun was the true cause of the seasons. We would
express this by saying that if the earth's axis were not tilted at 23 degrees to the vertical,
there would be no seasonal changes on the earth, for this tilt brings the regions of the
earth's surface into the sun's heat then out again in the course of the year.

One further type of celestial motion was observed by the Greeks and perhaps by
others too, namely that the whole starry sphere is slowly shifting westwards. The stars
drift in paths parallel to the ecliptic by about one degree in 72 years. The movement,
now known as the precession of the equinoxes, has important consequences for the later
mapping of the heavens and it will be referred to many times in this book. Its cause is
the slight perturbation of the earth's axis, whose poles are revolving slowly in a circle
with a radius of 23 degrees. A precessional cycle, carrying the stars round the sky
completely, would take almost 26,000 years. This movement renders an accurately-
drawn star chart valid only for a limited period of time, say 50–100 years. Its most
noticeable effect is that the pole star is only the pole star for a given epoch, until the
north pole moves gradually into a new alignment. The present pole star, Polaris, will be
most directly above the north pole in the year 2100AD. In the Old Kingdom of Egypt
(2500–2100)BC the star Thuban in the constellation Draco was the pole star, and some
pyramids appear to have been aligned with its historic position at that time.

In the evolution of genuine celestial maps, a reference co-ordinate system was
essential. The simplest is a horizon system where positions are given in altitudes degrees

BYLICA'S CELESTIAL GLOBE, 1480. Martin Bylica was a scientist and astrologer in Cracow from 1466 to 1493. He commissioned this globe from the instrument-maker Hans Dorn, and bequeathed it to the university. The earliest known western celestial globe, it is closely modelled on Islamic globes and is clearly related to the Vienna manuscript. Structurally, the large square horizon plate and the astrolabe mounted at the north pole are most unusual. The detached mounting of the meridian of longitude and the circle of latitude was recommended by Ptolemy in order to render the globe immune from precessional obsolescence.

Bibliotheka Jagiellonska, Poland

above the horizon plane, and in azimuth (direction) clockwise around the horizon starting from a predetermined point, for example due north. But it is clear that such a chart would be valid only for a given latitude, a certain season and indeed a particular time of night. It would be essentially a diagram of one part of the sky at one moment only, and a whole series of such maps would be required to cover a year, and even then they could be used only in their place of origin. These problems were to be addressed in the design of the astrolabe. A more comprehensive and objective system of star mapping is obviously desirable. The significance of the ecliptic is that it provided a baseline in an objective framework upon which the first maps or globes of the sky might be drawn.

Throughout late classical, medieval and early modern astronomy, celestial latitude was measured north or south of the ecliptic plane. Celestial longitude was measured east from the point where the ecliptic crosses the plane of the equator, known as the first point of Aries. This marked one of the great turning points of the year, the spring equinox which now takes place on or near March 21. At the time when the astrological star signs of the Zodiac originated, around 300BC, they coincided with the relevant constellations. But by the precessional movement described above, these constellations have now shifted some 30 degrees westward. The traditional signs of astrology have not been moved however, so that the 'sign of Aries' is now occupied by Pisces. The spring equinox will be contained in Pisces until *c.*2700AD when it will move into Aquarius. The following table illustrates this important point.

Constellation	Current Solar Passage	Containment of Vernal Equinox	Astrological Sign Period
Aries	Apr 19–May 14	2000BC–100BC	Mar 21–Apr 19
Taurus	May 15–June 20	4500BC–2000BC	Apr 20–May 20
Gemini	June 21–July 20	6600BC–4500BC	May 21–June 21
Cancer	July 21–Aug 10	8100BC–6600BC	June 22–July 22
Leo	Aug 11–Sept 16	10800BC–8100BC	July 23–Aug 22
Virgo	Sept 17–Oct 30	12000AD–15300AD	Aug 23–Sept 22
Libra	Nov 1–Nov 23	10300AD–12000AD	Sept 23–Oct 23
Scorpio	Nov 24–Dec 17	8600AD–10300AD	Oct 24–Nov 21
Sagitarius	Dec 18–Jan 19	6300AD–8600AD	Nov 22–Dec 21
Capricorn	Jan 20–Feb 15	4400AD–6300AD	Dec 22–Jan 19
Aquarius	Feb 16–Mar 11	2700AD–4400AD	Jan 20–Feb 18
Pisces	Mar 12–Apr 11	100BC–2700AD	Feb 19–Mar 20

The other fundamental requisite for celestial mapping was some form of zoning or landmarking to compensate for the absence of topography in the sky. The origin of constellations is a problem that belongs perhaps to the study of mythology and anthropology rather than astronomy; but the 88 star-groups now accepted by modern astronomers fall into fairly distinct historical groups, as the table overleaf shows:

The 88 Constellations with some Principal Stars

THE PTOLEMAIC CONSTELLATIONS: The Zodiac

ARIES	Ram	
TAURUS	Bull	Aldebaran, Pleiades
GEMINI	Twins	Castor, Pollux
CANCER	Crab	
LEO	Lion	Regulus
VIRGO	Virgin	Spica
LIBRA	Scales	
SCORPIUS	Scorpion	Antares
SAGITTARIUS	Archer	
CAPRICORN	Sea-Goat	
AQUARIUS	Water-Bearer	
PISCES	Fishes	

NORTHERN PTOLEMAIC CONSTELLATIONS:

ANDROMEDA	Andromeda	M31 galaxy
AQUILA	Eagle	Altair
AURIGA	Charioteer	Capella
BOÖTES	Herdsman	Arcturus
CASSIOPEIA	Cassiopeia	
CEPHEUS	Cepheus	
CORONA BOREALIS	Northern Crown	
CYGNUS	Swan	Deneb
DELPHINUS	Dolphin	
DRACO	Dragon	Thuban
EQUULEUS	Little Horse	
HERCULES	Hercules	
LYRA	Lyre (-bird)	Vega
OPHIUCHUS	Serpent-Handler	
PEGASUS	Winged Horse	
PERSEUS	Perseus	Algol
SAGITTA	Arrow	
SERPENS	Serpent	
TRIANGULUM	Triangle	
URSA MAJOR	Great Bear	
URSA MINOR	Little Bear	Polaris

SOUTHERN PTOLEMAIC CONSTELLATIONS:

ARA	Altar	
ARGO NAVIS	Ship	(Now divided into 4)
CANIS MAJOR	Great Dog	Sirius
CANIS MINOR	Little Dog	Procyon
CENTAURUS	Centaur	Alpha
CETUS	Whale	
CORONA AUSTRINA	Southern Crown	
CORVUS	Crow	
CRATER	Cup	
ERIDANUS	River	Achernar
HYDRA	Water Snake	
LEPUS	Hare	
LUPUS	Wolf	
ORION	Hunter	Rigel, Betelgeuse
PISCES AUSTRINUS	Southern Fish	Fomalhaut

SOUTHERN CONSTELLATIONS ADDED c.1600

APUS	Bird of Paradise	
CHAMELEON	Chameleon	
DORADO	Swordfish	Large Magellanic Cloud
GRUS	Crane	
HYDRUS	Water-Snake	
INDUS	Indian	
MUSCA	Fly	
PAVO	Peacock	
PHOENIX	Phoenix	
TRIANGULUM AUSTRALE	Southern Triangle	
		Small Magellanic Cloud
TUCANA	Toucan	
VOLANS	Flying Fish	

CONSTELLATIONS OF JAKOB BARTSCH, 1624

CAMELOPARDALIS	Giraffe
COLUMBA	Dove
MONOCEROS	Unicorn

CONSTELLATIONS OF HEVELIUS, 1687

CANES VENATICI	Hunting Dogs
LACERTA	Lizard
LEO MINOR	Small Lion
LYNX	Lynx
SCUTUM	Shield
SEXTANS	Sextant
VULPECULA	Fox

ANCIENT STAR GROUPS NOW REFORMED

CARINA	Keel of Ship	Canopus
COMA BERENICES	Berenice's Hair	
CRUX	Southern Cross	
PUPPIS	Stern of Ship	
PYXIS	Compass of Ship	
VELA	Sail of Ship	

SOUTHERN CONSTELLATIONS OF LACAILLE, c.1750

ANTLIA	Pump
CAELUM	Chisel
CIRCINUS	Compasses
FORNAX	Furnace
HOROLOGIUM	Clock
MENSA	Table
MICROSCOPIUM	Microscope
NORMA	Square
OCTANS	Octant
PICTOR	Easel
RETICULUM	Reticle
SCULPTOR	Sculptor's Workshop
TELESCOPIUM	Telescope

1
THE MOST ANCIENT SCIENCE

'Do you believe that the sciences would ever have arisen and
become great if there had not been before magicians,
alchemists, astrologers and wizards who thirsted
and hungered after hidden, forbidden powers?'

— Nietzsche *The Joyful Science*, 1886

'Odysseus
Gazing with fixed eye on the Pleiades,
Boötes setting late, and the Great Bear . . .
Looking ever towards Orion . . .'

Homer, *Odyssey*, Book V

THE HOMERIC POEMS ARE THE OLDEST CREATIONS of European literature, dating from not later than 800BC, yet the astronomical knowledge embodied in these lines is at least 1,000 years older still. Astronomy is by far the oldest exact science, fulfilling perfectly the simplest definition of science as knowledge of the natural world, its regularities and patterns. All ancient cultures observed the stars and recognized their cyclical changes. Through patient, naked-eye observation over centuries, practised star-watchers in Europe, Egypt, Mesopotamia, China and Central America built up a knowledge of the sky that was far more detailed than their knowledge of the world in which they lived. In ancient societies, indeed in all pre-industrial societies, real darkness still filled much of men's lives, and the farmer, priest or seafarer was familiar with the star-patterns as the fundamental gauges of time and direction. All cultures have identified star groupings, constellations, in the sky. Their resemblance to their supposed subjects was often tenuous, but they were essentially mnemonic devices serving to unify groups of stars, and impose some order on the ocean of the night sky.

Yet alongside this precise, observed regularity, was another very different element: the sense of the mystery of the sky, that it was a realm quite other than this earth, a realm where divinities, and spirits had their home, for the most part dwelling in icy serenity, but not infrequently unleashing storms, and exercising a mysterious power to shape men's lives. It is this duality of precise observation and religious awe that gives the early history of astronomy a double fascination. In the ancient near east, where recorded astronomy begins, the agency of gods or demons was seen in every aspect of life and nature. Mesopotamian civilization perceived in the sky one of the most fundamental patterns of nature, for the sky was the great time-measurer: the alternation of day and night, sun and moon, summer and winter, divided and regulated the endless flow of time. All this was recorded and mastered in detail. Yet beneath these observed patterns there has always been the search for causes. The causes advanced by thinkers throughout much of human history would now be rejected as illusory: the overwhelming cause assigned by pre-critical science was the will of the gods. But even the gods did not offer a universal escape from the exercise of reason, for the question inevitably arose whether the gods and spirits wielded arbitrary, irrational power, or whether they too obeyed fundamental rules. All ancient cultures, except perhaps the Chinese, regarded the heavenly bodies as divine, and their regularity and serenity, so different from the striving and suffering of human life, seemed to hint at a fundamental order lying at the heart of nature. This co-existence of science and religion can be seen in many creation myths in which the crucial element is the imposition of order on primal chaos. In the Babylonian creation epic *Enuma Elish* (*c*.1800–1500BC), Marduk kills the unruly goddess of primal waters, Thiamat, and cuts her body in two, using one half to create the heavens and the other as the earth. The constellations, the movement of sun and moon, were to be under Marduk's beneficent rule, and to mark the passage of time. Such myths reveal a sense of, or perhaps search for, order in the universe, amid numerous elements of chaos. This same order-seeking impulse lay behind the cosmic diagrams drawn in many ancient cultures, which depicted some of the fundamental elements of earth and sky and sought to locate man in space and time.

The very earliest evidence of astronomical awareness is older still, but is more

STONE CIRCLE, Old Keig, Aberdeenshire. A pattern of stone monument characteristic of north-east Scotland: the recumbent stone between the two uprights clearly formed an artificial horizon over which the sun, moon or stars could be observed at some significant point in their orbit or elevation.
Crown Copyright. By Courtesy of R.C.A.H.M.S., Edinburgh

difficult to interpret. Many of the megalithic stone structures of northern Europe are unmistakably aligned with heavenly bodies, and with a precision that argues for a mature tradition of observation. Stonehenge's alignment with the midsummer sunrise is the most famous, and a well-developed calendar, and perhaps also some form of sun-cult, must be assumed among the people who built and used Stonehenge. Such stone or earth structures were built in order to create an artificial horizon against which astronomical events could be precisely observed; they were in a sense instruments. Some of these instruments are aligned on objects more subtle and surprising than the sun: in north-east Scotland there are stone-groups in a recurrent pattern of two erect columns framing a horizontal, recumbent stone, which makes a clear, level horizon. Some of these stones appear to register the upper and lower limits of the moon's orbital plane, a movement which occupies an eighteen-year cycle, and it seems impossible that these alignments could be accidental. These stones probably date from around 2000BC onwards, and if they have been correctly interpreted they argue a degree of sophistication in their builders' knowledge of the skies that is truly startling, and one which must have been built up over centuries of painstaking observation. There are many still more enigmatic examples too. The so-called White Horse at Uffington in Berkshire, a figure cut into the chalk hillside, may not be a horse at all, since it appears to be connected with the constellation Taurus, and with the rising of the bright star Aldebaran — 'the eye of Taurus' — over the animal figure. In the absence of archaeological or written records, it is impossible to interpret such sites or to infer the true motives of the ancient astronomers. The most likely explanation of such alignments is that they were gauges of time: when the moon or sun or a certain star reached a predetermined position, it was known that the year had elapsed and that the cycle would begin again. But how and why were the complex cycles of more than a year studied and interpreted? They clearly might form part of a belief system in which the order which the observers found in the heavens was indicative of something fundamental, if mysterious, in the universe. The roots of astronomy have always been both practical and religious: it was studied and used, and it fed the mind and the imagination.

ANCIENT ASTRONOMY

The crucial practical use to which astronomy was put, and which provides evidence of observational traditions in virtually all ancient cultures, was the making of calendars. It was widely noticed that the basic time-units of the day and the year did not precisely divide, the one into the other, and moreover that the intermediate unit, the lunar month, did not match with the solar cycle. All the complexities of the calendar result from these irreconcilable time periods. All cultures have sought to find greater time periods or cycles in which these three would coincide, before diverging again. Such a cycle could be used to tie days, years, dynasties, eclipses and religious ceremonies into a greater historical framework. Some of the ancient cycles occupied centuries or even millenia, and their calculation involved observing the stars and planets over many generations, and required powerful mathematical systems to extend the results far into the future. For example the Egyptian civil calendar adopted the round figure of 365 days for a year early in the third millenium BC. But since the natural year is actually closer to 365.25 days the civil calendar began to creep slowly forward through the natural year. The Egyptians noticed this and calculated correctly that in 1460 years the calendar would coincide with the true sidereal year, the year of the star-cycle. This was known as the Sothic cycle, after the bright star Sothis, known to us as Sirius, which played a vital part in their year.

But however sophisticated their calendars, these ancient sciences have left almost no evidence of their work in graphic form: there are no genuine star charts extant from ancient Mesopotamia, Egypt, India, China, or Mexico. Pictures and diagrams, some childishly simple, others more complex, are all that have survived. These ancient societies had not developed cartographic awareness or a cartographic language in general, in relation to terrestrial mapping, so that it would be unreasonable to expect the concept of mapping to be applied to the heavens. In all pre-Hellenic sciences, it seems that the key which would underlie accurate celestial mapping — that of spherical geometry — was absent. If they proposed models of the cosmos or diagrams of parts of the heavens, they were figurative, poetic and without serious spatial structure. Lore, tradition, and oral wisdom were paramount in these societies, and, to the priestly elite who studied the skies, elementary diagrams of the star positions would have served no purpose. The other important area in which no specific evidence has survived is ancient navigation. Literary references in Homer show clearly that Mediterranean sailors used the sun and stars, especially the pole star, for direction-finding, but their skills were undoubtedly handed down through oral tradition rather than documents or maps. When seafaring lore was first written down, the earliest graphic form to emerge was not the star-map but the wind-rose, a type of compass whose points were the four or eight winds, for the skilled mariner could readily distinguish between the cold northerly wind and the warm southerly, and set his course accordingly.

EGYPTIAN CONSTELLATIONS from the tomb of Seti 1, c.1275BC. These northern constellations appear in various contexts in Egyptian art. The only certain identification that can be made is the Ox and his Handler, where our Plough (Ursa Major) can be clearly seen. The unfamiliar hippopotamus, crocodile, and the falcon-headed god Horus do not correspond to any classical constellation. These star-groups would later be integrated with the Babylonian Zodiac figures.

THE FOUNDATIONS OF ASTRONOMY:
EGYPT AND BABYLON

Despite this absence of graphic images which we would recognize as star maps, there is ample evidence of astronomical science contemporary with the neolithic structures of northern Europe, and with the invention of writing in Mesopotamia and Egypt in the third millenium BC, it becomes possible to interpret both knowledge and beliefs. In Egypt as early as the Old Kingdom (c.2500–2100BC) a form of stellar reference system had been devised, to which the term Decans was later applied. The Decans were 36 star groups in the vicinity of which the sun rose in the course of a year. They functioned effectively as a constellation system, as landmarks in the sky, and their appearance as decorations on temple ceilings, tombs and coffin lids may be considered the oldest astronomical pictures in the world, although whether they can be regarded as genuine maps is a matter of debate. The Decans became associated with various deities and are represented as individual figures, as are the planets. The Decans were all in a band just south of the ecliptic, but other major northern constellations became fixed too and recur in recognizable form in paintings spread over many centuries. The striking thing about

them is that, with a very few exceptions, they cannot be identified with the classical constellations with which we are familiar. This tends to upset any belief that the constellations are in any sense objective or inevitable. The planets however seem always to have been regarded as personal deities, as they were in most other cultures, and are shown as animal-headed gods upright in the boats in which they journeyed through the night. 'Horus the Red' is clearly Mars, while 'The Crosser' with two faces is Venus, recognized as both the morning and evening star.

The Egyptian civil calendar was built around the decans, which formed 36 'weeks' each of ten days, with five intercalary days added to complete the year. In Egypt the turning points of the solar year, the summer and winter solstices, lacked the importance they carried for more northerly cultures. Instead the annual flooding of the river Nile in July was the crucial event which irrigated the land, and this was seen to coincide with the first appearance each year of the star Sirius (in Egypt Sothis) after its period of invisibility below the horizon. Thus the festival of Sothis each summer was the year's great turning point, in the month called 'The Opener of the Year'. This first pre-dawn rising of a star after the period during which it rose in daylight is known as heliacal rising, and it was an important concept to the early Egyptians. Each day after its heliacal rising, a star would rise slightly more in advance of the sun, until another suitably conspicuous star rose heliacally. The decans centred around such stars, and the Egyptian map of the heavens hinged on this concept of star rising, which in an intriguing way also left its mark on the hour divisions of the day and night. The Egyptians were deeply interested in the passage of the sun-god Re through the underworld at night, on his ship with his attendant deities before his re-emergence in triumph each dawn. The underworld was considered to be divided into twelve regions in each of which he spent a short period of time. To measure these periods the nightly rising of twelve stars was fixed upon, and the interval between them was termed an hour, the hieroglyph for which is a star. From this system the Egyptians devised star clocks which appear on many coffin-lids from 2200BC onwards. They take the form of columns of star names for each hour of the night and for each decanal week of the year, so that by matching the star seen rising in the sky with its symbol in the table, the sky became to the skilled observer literally a clock. It is interesting to note that this type of star clock vanished *c.*1500BC, presumably because

BABYLONIAN SUN GOD: Shamash is seen sawing his way up through the eastern mountains, with Ishtar (Venus) goddess of the morning star before him. Rivers, in the form of Ea, god of fresh water, run down from the mountains, *c.*2300BC.
British Museum, Department of Western Asiatic Antiquities

those who needed to do so had mastered this symbolic map and could read the hours directly from a glance at the sky. The twelve hour division of the day was apparently purely by analogy with the night, and shadow clocks were marked with five divisions: the shadow crossed the five markers as it shortened towards noon, then recrossed them as it lengthened towards evening, with one hour of twilight both for sunrise and for sunset.

The cult of the sun left its mark on the architecture of Egypt as it did on that of northern Europe. The temple of Amun-Re, the sun-god, at Karnak was aligned so that the setting sun shone through an axis corridor into the sanctuary of the temple. The celebrated apostate king Akhenaton (1353–1356BC) instituted a new monotheistic worship of the sun, and his new palace at Amarna was richly decorated with scenes of sun-worship. The new cult further stimulated astronomical observation, but it was short-lived, dying with the king himself. The astronomical significance of the pyramids themselves is uncertain. The alignment of shafts in the Giza pyramids with the ancient pole-star Thuban (in the constellation Draco) has been established, but the motive remains obscure. For all their evident scientific skills, the Egyptians left no precise records of astronomical observations, no star catalogue, no tables of star risings, planetary movements, eclipses and so on. Nor did they devise anything in the nature of astronomical theory: there was apparently no speculation, scientific or religious, as to the causes of what they observed in the sky. Instead Egyptian astronomy was intensely practical, whether that practicality was in the field of time-measurement or divination.

The true origins of classical astronomy lay elsewhere in the ancient near east, in

15

Mesopotamia, where detailed observations and calculations were first recorded, and where it becomes possible for us to recover a system of beliefs about the heavens. Some of the mathematical methods of the Babylonians were extremely powerful and sophisticated; the constellations they designated proved permanent, and their philosophical view of man's relation to the cosmos laid the foundations of astrology.

The very earliest explicitly astronomical texts are Babylonian, dating from *c.*1500–1700BC. They are clay tablets written in the cuneiform script, and they take the form of omens in which the positions of sun, moon, stars and planets are related to events such as wars, famines, and royal successions. Thus these earliest texts make the fundamental

BABYLONIAN SCENE WITH PLEIADES, *c.*800BC. The seven stars are clearly visible in the sky above this hunting scene. Despite the Babylonians' immense astronomical skills, they left virtually no visual images of the skies, and the concept of maps or diagrams of the heavens was apparently unknown to them.
British Museum, Department of Western Asiatic Antiquities

link between the precise science of astronomical observation and the art of divination, the two forces that were to motivate astronomy for the next 3,000 years. So deep was this early interest in divination that one of the strongest motives for the constant observation of the sky was the hope of obtaining warnings of future events in nature and in human life. In this early period the Zodiac does not appear; the moon, planets and some constellations form the material basis of the omens. Star figures such as the Lion, Bull and Scorpion make their earliest appearance here, and they appear in Babylonian sculptures in other contexts too. It is interesting to note that the brightest stars in these groups, together with that of Pegasus, are almost exactly 90 degrees apart on the Zodiac circle, and their heliacal risings coincide with the four turning points of the year: the spring equinox, summer solstice, autumn equinox and winter solstice. This suggests that the framework at least of the Zodiac structure had already been recognized. The omens however are based on visible events current in the sky, not on calculations of invisible influences. The stars were termed 'the gods of the night', while the sun was depicted as a regal figure rising each dawn from a mountain range. At this early stage the Babylonians, like the Egyptians, seem to have believed that the sun passed each night in an underworld, where the stars probably stayed during the day.

From this earliest date the Babylonians identified the heavenly bodies as in themselves divinities able to affect human life. Indeed the belief in the *personality* of the heavenly bodies was the essential starting-point for what was later to become astrology. It was the deities themselves, such as Marduk or Ishtar (corresponding to Jupiter and Venus) who might determine matters of politics or love, and their will was thought to be discernible through their celestial behaviour. The notion that the planets could control human events *as planets*, by virtue of their astronomical position alone, is secondary, and it is also far less rational. The prediction of human events by planetary position depended on an exact knowledge of the heavens, but paradoxically the later accumulation of that knowledge served to obscure the original belief in the personality of the celestial deities. Once the personal aspect of heavenly bodies is lost sight of, the crucial question prompted by these omens, by the belief in celestial divination, is whether the stars and planets actually cause events or merely indicate that they will happen? It is possible to see astrology as a belief system appropriate to a wholly mechanistic universe where man has no free will, and where perhaps the divine powers are also fixed in their roles. This vision would later present grave difficulties for all the mature religions. In the early Babylonian phase, the omens, as manipulated by the priesthood, functioned mainly to guide the court in matters of politics, war and personal fortune. They seem to have been regarded as indicative only, not as revealing inexorable fate, so that religious observances and magic might avert the omen. The Assyrian king Esarhaddon (690–669BC) was so fearful of lunar eclipses that during his reign he enthroned substitute king-figures when eclipses occured, who were afterwards executed to divert the malign influence of the eclipse from the king himself. The Babylonians' skills in astronomy and their astral religion both left their mark on the Old Testament: the prophets' horror of star-worship is expressed by Isaiah: 'Let now the astrologers, the stargazers, the monthly prognosticators, stand up and save thee from these things that shall come upon thee. Behold they shall be as stubble; the fire shall burn them . . .'.

Despite such deep levels of superstition, Babylonian astronomy was based on rigorous observation and on advanced mathematical skills. Like all ancient civilizations their observations were made only with the naked eye, but they built structures which functioned as artificial horizons with fixed observation points, which may be considered as early instruments. Detailed computations of stellar and planetary motions formed the basis of their calendars, as they did later of the art of astrology. Remarkably, the Babylonians developed no form of spherical geometry or trigonometry: celestial positions and timings were all predicted mathematically, and the concepts of star maps or cosmic models were apparently quite unknown. The method used to achieve this was to record the times at which a heavenly body appeared at two or more cardinal points, then to calculate all its further positions as *functions of time* in constant progression. Allowance was made for the changing velocities of the planets, which the Babylonians were able to tabulate in almanacs. This method was applied with precision and sophistication, and led to what was probably the most important development in classical astronomy: the designation of the Zodiac. It had already been noticed that the sun dwelt for three months in each quarter of a celestial circle marked by the cardinal points Scorpio, Leo, Taurus, and (at that time) Pegasus. If each of these sky-regions were further divided into three, corresponding to the months of year, the sun's position in each of twelve signs of the Zodiac was formalized. Pegasus's place was more accurately filled by Aquarius, and each sign occupied thirty degrees, corresponding to the thirty days in each month.

This division of the sky into twelve and the ability to plot celestial positions led to a quickening development of astrology from the fifth century BC onwards. The aspects of the heavens could now be formalized: the movements of the planets — the personal deities whose influence was so important — through the Zodiac, and characteristics of the Zodiac figures could be elaborated into a psychological drama into which the human subject stepped to play his part. The generalized predictions of the omens were replaced by the archetypal form of astrology, the horoscope, which derives from the situation of the heavenly bodies at a precise moment, that situation being known and charted long before or long after the moment itself. A complex network of influences involving the entire heavenly sphere, visible and invisible, could now be plotted, clearly a more sophisticated concept than the earlier omen system. It is difficult to believe that such a significant exercise in zoning did not result in the creation of some type of map or model, whether in two dimensions or three, but if they were made in ancient Mesopotamia, they have not survived. From this zoning sprang, later, the most important innovation in man's charting of the sky, the concept of a co-ordinate system to locate heavenly bodies, using the ecliptic and celestial poles as fixed points from which to measure any position in the sky. When and where this crucial step was taken is uncertain; the Babylonians themselves seem not to have used a co-ordinate system as we know it, but by the third century BC the Babylonian Zodiac was known in Greece, where, plotted within the emerging rules of spherical geometry, it produced the classical form of celestial latitude and longitude which we understand today.

ASTRONOMY BEYOND EUROPE

Beyond Europe and the Near East the same imperatives of time-measurement and divination produced quite independent astronomical traditions. In China by 1000 BC the state maintained astronomers to draw up calendars, keep time, interpret omens and monitor weather conditions, and this state-supported science reached a high degree of observational precision. It seems possible from the references of later astronomers that star charts of some sort were in existence in China by the fourth century BC. These have not survived, but a fully worked-out star catalogue listing 1464 stars in 284 constellations was drawn up by Chhien Lu-Chih in the fifth century AD. The oldest extant two-dimensional star map from any civilization, the Dunhuang manuscript from the tenth century AD, clearly belongs within a mature tradition of celestial mapping. On a more philosophical level, there was in China a marked absence of cosmological modelling, and no impulse to people the cosmos with deities and demons. Chinese philosophy apparently did not conceive of a creator-god standing outside his created world, and Chinese science was not drawn to rationalize the laws of nature or causation, whether the causation of physics or of the divine will. Instead the prevailing concern, whether of Confucian pragmatism or Taoist mysticism, was the organic wholeness of the universe. This wholeness could be grasped intuitively through the perception of nature's balanced forces Yin and Yang, manifest in the antithesis of day and night, male and female, sun and moon, hot and cold, and so on. Such a 'worship of the universe through the worship of its parts' produced a cast of thought very different from the synthesizing rationalism of western science.

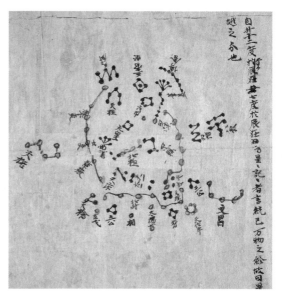

CHINESE STAR CHART, 940AD. The oldest surviving paper star map from any civilization. The Great Bear is visible on the left, and the chains of stars around the north pole were conceived as analogous to the walls of the Imperial Palace: that is in Chinese thought they enclosed the pivotal region of the universe.

The British Library, O.I.O.C. Stein 332b

By contrast the ancient astronomy of Central America, equally precocious in exact observation, was used to underpin an exuberant cult of deities, demons and cosmic imagery. The Aztec, and even more the Maya peoples developed the ability to analyze astronomical events mathematically and to predict events with great accuracy. Their calendar-making advanced beyond time measurement into the designation of an elaborate cycle of unique identifiable days, extending over 52 years, or 18,980 days, called a Calendar Round, after which it repeated itself. Each day was regarded as possessing a certain fateful character derived from the ascendant stars. Personal astrology in the western sense did not develop, but the reading of astral omens became an essential priestly function. Their elaboration in almanacs belongs perhaps to the history of anthropology rather than astronomy, but the central cults of the sun and Venus (as the male god Quetzacoatl) were underpinned by rigorous observation over many centuries. Highly animistic pictures of the sun and other gods are common, but there is nothing in the nature of star maps. The Central American cultures had not developed the science of geometry, and spherical geometry in particular, which was the key to cosmic modelling, was unknown. Instead they seem to have conceived of a flat, layered

MAYA CALDENDAR STELE from Seibal, Guatamala. It was the Maya practice to erect such stone effigies to commemorate rulers, events, or time-periods and they were always precisely dated. This one is dated to 28 November AD 849. No other cultures felt the need to record the passage of time in such a monumental, public way.
Photo: Norman Hammond

universe, each layer the domain of one kind of celestial body — clouds, moon, sun, stars, comets, planets, and in the final layer resided the creator-god. This system clearly precluded any attempt to grapple with the dynamics of astral motion. It is striking that the Central American cultures, like the Mesopotamian, developed sophisticated mathematical astronomy, but left so little graphic record of their science.

In India the ancient Vedic literature, dating from c.1500–1200BC, is full of references to astral gods, and to the balance of cosmic forces both before and after the world's creation. There is no evidence of mathematical techniques of astronomy in India before the fifth century BC. One distinctive feature of the Indian perception of the sky was a celestial reference system relating not to the sun but to the moon — the *naksatras*, the lunar mansions — which was established by 800BC. In this system it was the position of the moonrise against the night sky which defined a series of star groupings. Although simpler than calculating the sun's position against invisible stars, it was not destined to replace the Zodiac outside India; yet the system had a long and involved history and formed an important feature in astrology, eastern and western. From the fifth century BC onwards, classical Indian astronomy developed under a series of influences from the west, from Mesopotamia, Persia, Greece, and Islam. Key texts from these foreign sources were translated into Sanskrit, and Indian astronomers embraced the Babylonian Zodiac, Aristotelian cosmology, the Ptolemaic star catalogue and Hellenistic astrology. In the cosmology of the Puranas (popular encyclopedic literature c.400–800AD) a series of wheels bearing the heavenly bodies revolves above the earth, their axis in the sacred mountain Meru, their motive power the breath of Brahma, a vision clearly rooted in Greek cosmology, but not one worked out in terms of spherical geometry. Indian wisdom was essentially other-worldly, focusing on ways of escape from the mechanism of fate and the cycle of action and suffering, and in this world astrology became central. While star maps in the strict sense were unknown in classical India, there was an exuberant tradition of cosmological charting and modelling, in which human life was represented in pictures together with the elements of the natural and spiritual realms.

MEXICAN ASTRONOMER. A priest or astronomer is seen watching the seven stars of the Pleiades, c.1300AD.
Bodleian Library, Oxford, MS Arch. Seld.A.1.f.12

GREEK SCIENCE FROM HOMER
TO PTOLEMY

Contemporary with the mature phase of Babylonian astronomy — the designation of the Zodiac and the incipient art of astrology — the foundations of a dramatically new and different scientific tradition were being laid in Greece. From the earliest Greek philosopher-scientists whose names have come down to us — Thales, Anaximander, Pythagoras, etc. — there is a decisive shift in approach towards a critical, analytical scientific spirit. The universe is regarded as a rational structure, capable of yielding its secrets to logical thought and inquiry. The will of the gods was no longer adequate to explain the forces of nature and the phenomena which man observed, and instead secular explanations were sought which satisfied the questioning intellect. Fundamental questions such as the nature of matter were addressed for the first time. The central problem which came to dominate Greek astronomy was that of the structure of the cosmos: what model could explain the motions of the heavenly bodies in relation to the earth? This had never been addressed as a theoretical problem by the Babylonians or Egyptians, and it was the Hellenic skill with geometry, especially spherical geometry, that explains their progress in this area. It has to be emphasized that no celestial maps or diagrams of any kind have survived from the classical Greek period, but their approach and their achievement are recorded in some detail in a number of important texts.

Traditional Greek lore, as preserved in Homer for example, saw the sky as a dome of iron or bronze supported by pillars over a static and probably flat earth. By the fourth century BC however, Parmenides had satisfied himself that the earth was a sphere, and that the moon shone with reflected sunlight, while Empedocles was probably the first to interpret correctly the geometry of solar eclipses. One of the seminal influences was

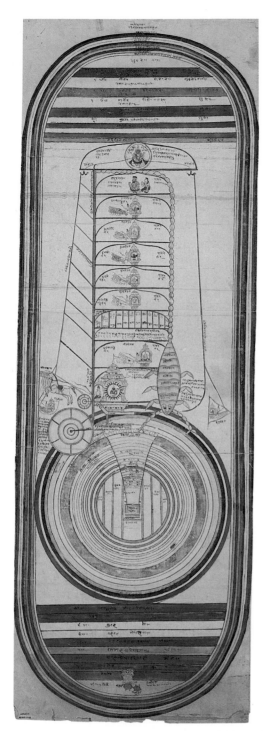

INDIAN COSMOLOGICAL CHART. Although dated *c*.1750, from South India, this painting represents a Hindu tradition of cosmological chart that reaches back almost 2,000 years. The central earth and the ten upper layers of heaven and the lower levels of hell are comprehensible enough. The intriguing thing about this chart is the vertical depth given to the universe, and the distinct realms of the seven personified planets, which clearly betray the influence of western classical astronomy.

Victoria and Albert Museum, London

probably Pythagoras's teaching concerning the perfection of the figure of the sphere, a perfection that was both physical and metaphysical. This was typical of the Greek ability to handle an abstract, almost intuitive concept, and to build logical conclusions from it. For the Pythagoreans, it followed from this belief that the earth must possess the most perfect form known to nature, the sphere, and that the heavens which surround the earth must also share this spherical structure. But Greek astronomers were also aware that as one travelled north or south, different stars rose into view while others dropped below the opposite horizon. Unless the stars were very close, this could only be explained if the earth's surface were curved, so that there were good empirical, as well as philosophical, reasons for regarding both the earth and the surrounding heavens as spheres. Later Greek scientists and philosophers all became convinced that spherical motion held the key to the structure of the cosmos. It was on this aspect of the mapping of the heavens — the structural rather than the locational — that Greek science expended so much thought and had such long-lasting influence. It is difficult to over-emphasize the importance of the concept of the heavenly sphere: it provided a structure — a plane surface — upon which stellar positions could be measured and mapped according to the laws of geometry. This provided the basis for all serious celestial mapping, and it incidentally provided Greek geographers with a model for terrestrial mapmaking to.

The motions of the stars and planets, sun and moon, were each clearly regular, but they were far from uniform with each other. The retrograde motions of Mercury and Venus in particular offered a long-standing enigma: what model could explain the mysterious pattern of their movements, and what mechanism supported them and the other heavenly bodies in the sky? In the *Republic*, Plato relates the myth of a man killed in battle whose soul travels the regions of the spirit world. He is granted a vision of the cosmic structure as a nest of concentric hoops encircling a central axis, each hoop bearing a planet. The earth is a kind of spindle at the centre of the figure, and the hoops are turned by the Fates. In a later work, the *Timaeus*, Plato again describes the universe as a series of circular bands around the earth. Some scholars have argued that these texts are so graphic that Plato must have had before him a three-dimensional model of the heavens, like an armillary sphere, or even a mechanical model. More than a century after Plato wrote, Archimedes is reliably reported to have built such models. Plato gave expression to the Greek fixation with the sphere: 'Therefore the creator fashioned the world a rounded, spherical shape with the extremes equidistant in all directions, a figure that has the greatest degree of completeness and uniformity . . . and he established a single, spherical universe in circular motion.'

It was an exact contemporary of Plato, Eudoxus of Cnidus, who first articulated a theory of cosmic structure based on circular motion with the earth at the centre of 26 circular bands bearing the sun, moon, stars and planets. Why 26? Because each celestial body has a double or even triple motion — the daily rotation and the yearly cycle — which could be explained only by a spherical orbit which bore upon itself the centre of a second motion. The elaboration of these two elements of the system became central to Greek cosmology. The general approach to cosmic structure advanced by Eudoxus acquired immense historical importance because it was shared by Aristotle and Ptolemy, and with their authority it became the accepted and dominant cosmic model in western thought for almost 1,500 years until the Copernican revolution. Eudoxus's second great achievement as an astronomer was the construction of the first recorded celestial globe, depicting the constellations within a co-ordinate framework of the ecliptic and tropics, the poles and the equator. This clearly drew upon an established corpus of observations, and was influential in fixing the classical constellations, which have remained unaltered ever since. It is certain that Babylonian knowledge had reached Greece by this time

THE FARNESE ATLAS. The oldest surviving celestial globe, and the only map of the heavens from Greek and Roman antiquity. Although the sculpture dates from the second century AD it was undoubtedly copied from earlier models, and it embodies the astronomy of Eudoxus and Hipparchus. No individual stars are shown, but most of the classical constellations are clearly visible; they are shown as reversed images, in the 'classically-correct' style, as if seen from outside the celestial sphere.

Photograph: Scala

since the Babylonian Zodiac was included. Like all future celestial globes, the starry sphere is described and envisaged as seen from *the outside*, from some imaginary point in space beyond the cosmos. The practical difficulties of constructing concave or dome-like hemispheres to be viewed from inside were obviously too great; but moreover there was no conceptual obstacle for the Greeks in looking at the stars from 'outside space', since the starry sphere was conceived literally as a material but translucent sphere, located at a specific distance from the earth, on which the stars were carried. It was assumed that each of the other heavenly bodies was also borne on its own crystalline sphere, revolving independently inside each other. The depiction of the constellations from the outside had the important effect of reversing the figure-images: the zodiac progresses anti-clockwise around the ecliptic, and the head of Taurus, for example, faces to the right on the globe, but to the observer on earth it faces left. This became an established convention, and virtually all celestial globes down to the present day have been drawn as if from outside the stars. Eudoxus's globe has not survived, but it was undoubtedly the prototype of a series of Greek celestial globes, and the Farnese Atlas, a celestial globe carved in stone dating from the second century AD is its direct descendent.

Eudoxus's original text was rewritten in verse around 250BC by the poet Aratus of Soli, and the resulting work, the *Phaenomena*, became one of the most popular scientific texts in the classical, post-classical and medieval worlds. Since Eudoxus's own work is lost, Aratus's poem is the oldest known systematic account of the classical constellations. Their appearance and location are given in perhaps 10–20 lines of rather rhetorical verse, and reference is made to the mythical background of the figures. The planets are also described, and although the cosmic structure is not elaborated in any detail, a system of geocentric circles may be deduced from what Aratus says. The positions of the planets in the constellations is used to give a series of detailed weather predictions, but no personal astrology enters into the poem. Aratus's poem is a precise verbal description of 40 fairly simple visual images, and it is hard to believe that texts of the poem would not, from its earliest appearance, have been illustrated with a series of constellation-pictures.

Aristotle echoed the Greek preoccupation with spheres and circular motion as marks of perfection in nature. Aristotle divided the cosmos into the sublunary realm where all matter was composed of the four elements earth, air, fire and water, and the celestial

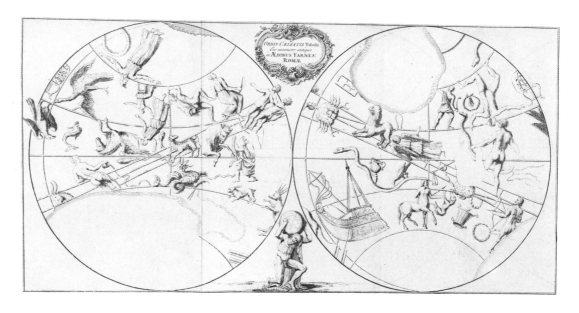

THE FARNESE ATLAS REDRAWN, from a printed edition of Manilius's *Astronomicon*, 1739.
The British Library, 685.h.2

realms where the unique fifth element not found on earth, the ether, reigns. Linear, irregular or intermittent motion characterizes things on earth, while the heavens are qualitatively different. This metaphysical, almost spiritualized, science is further reinforced by Aristotle's doctrine that all motion is caused, and caused constantly: anything that moves perpetually, as the sun or stars do, is perpetually being moved, and the motions of the heavens he ascribed to a prime mover. This *primum mobile* can be conceived as operating in the outermost sphere of the heavens, and each inner sphere was somehow 'geared' to its neighbour. By adding these differential, or counteracting, spheres, needed to isolate each sphere from the motion of the next, Aristotle increased the total number of spheres to 55. The mysterious prime mover, itself unmoved and eternal, became the subject of theological speculation, and the Aristotelian cosmic structure was found acceptable to Christianity for well over 1,000 years. Aristotle's authority also reinforced the enduring idea that the earth is stationary: both our senses and our logic tell us that the earth is vast and too heavy to move.

The early high-point of this rigorous intellectual science came with the work of Hipparchus (active 150–130BC), the most important astronomer before Ptolemy. His own works have not survived, but their contents are known from detailed references to him

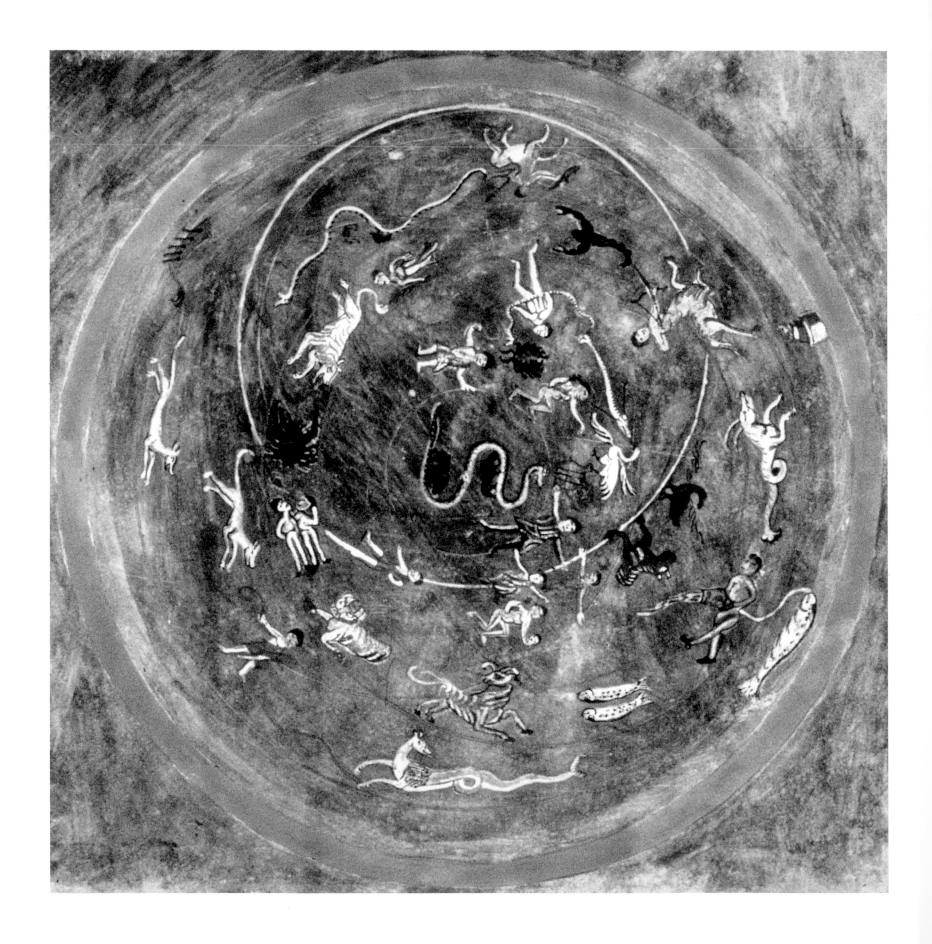

MITHRA. Stone relief, second century AD. The cult of the Persian sun-god Mithra spread throughout the later Roman Empire. Here Mithra slays the bull who was transformed into the moon, while Mithra's cloak became the heavens — the twelve Zodiac signs are plainly visible. The bull-sacrifice is of very ancient origin and may have been connected with spring fertility myths: until *c.*2000BC the vernal equinox lay within the constellation Taurus.
Städtisches Museum, Wiesbaden

ARATUS'S NORTHERN HEAVENS, from a Carolingian manuscript, 818AD. No contemporary illustrations of astronomy survive from the classical period itself, but illustrated copies of Aratus's *Phenomena* were made throughout the middle ages. The constellation figures are shown in their natural position, face-forward, with the Zodiac progressing clockwise, in contrast to the classical tradition of the Farnese globe.
Bayerische Staatsbibliothek, Munich

by Strabo and by Ptolemy himself. He pioneered the application of trigonometry to celestial calculations; he developed an early form of astrolabe; he constructed a star globe, and experimented with celestial co-ordinate systems. He understood clearly the relationships involved in eclipses, used parallax geometry to calculate accurately the distance from the earth to the moon, and he appreciated that the sun was vastly more distant, beyond his measuring ability. His most famous observational discovery was what later came to be called precession: he noticed that star positions are not absolutely fixed, but that the whole starry sphere moves slowly westward around the ecliptic. He was unable to measure this movement with great accuracy, but he put it at around one degree in a century (the true figure is 50 seconds of an arc each year, or one degree in 72 years). Hipparchus was not able to account for this motion, but he realized that its effect was to render any star maps or catalogues giving star positions valid for only a certain epoch, perhaps for half a century, depending on the accuracy the observer aims at. Hipparchus's prodigious skill as an observer was summed up in his pioneering star catalogue, listing 850 stars with their co-ordinates, and classified into six magnitudes of brightness. Hipparchus did not elaborate on the prevailing concentric cosmic model of Greek science, but he found no reason to quarrel with it. His approach to astronomy was precise, empirical and mathematical, and it seems certain that he made celestial maps, diagrams and globes for his own use; but, as with classical maps of all kinds, they have perished. For almost three centuries no other astronomer approached Hipparchus's originality and precision.

It was Ptolemy of Alexandria (active 130–160AD) who both summed up the achievement of classical science, and established the canon of astronomical knowledge for the following 1,400 years. In the introduction to his great book, the *Syntaxis*, better known by its later Arabic title the *Almagest*, Ptolemy advances an interesting, almost religious, plea for the study of astronomy. Moral insight, he argues, can grow from our reflecting on our worldly affairs; sciences such as physics and medicine deal with the changing, corruptible material world; but astronomy alone leads to a deep knowledge of the universe, focusing as it does on the eternal heavenly bodies, the motion of the cosmos, and the divine first mover. Ptolemy revised Hipparchus's star catalogue and expanded it to include 1,022 stars (including the few nebulae visible to the naked eye) with co-ordinates and degrees of magnitude. These stars and the 48 constellations in which they were grouped formed the basic material of all astronomy in the western world until the early seventeenth century. More dominant even than Augustine in theology or Virgil in literature, Ptolemy's authority as the guide to all things astronomical was paramount throughout the medieval and Renaissance world, and the *Almagest* was probably in continuous practical use longer than any other book in history, with the exception of Euclid's geometry. The concept of plotting positions on the celestial sphere by means of co-ordinates, as it was developed by Eudoxus, Hipparchus and Ptolemy, was transferred to the earthly sphere, and formed the basis of the late classical theory of mapmaking. No less important was Ptolemy's restatement of the circular cosmic model. In great geometric detail, Ptolemy calculated the motions of the planets, sun, moon, and starry sphere, each with interlocking cycles to represent daily and yearly revolution. He went further than his predecessors in stating that the universe could contain no empty space, and that the sphere of each heavenly body could not overlap another. He was able to calculate the distance of the moon from the earth, and therefore to estimate the total size of the cosmos. His figure, in several millions of miles, seemed sufficiently large to be plausible without raising disturbing problems connected with infinity, or with cosmic immensity as we now know them: the universe was vast but not too vast. Thus he portrayed the universe as a finite, closed system, a vision which satisfied both the intellect and the faith of Europe for more than a millenium.

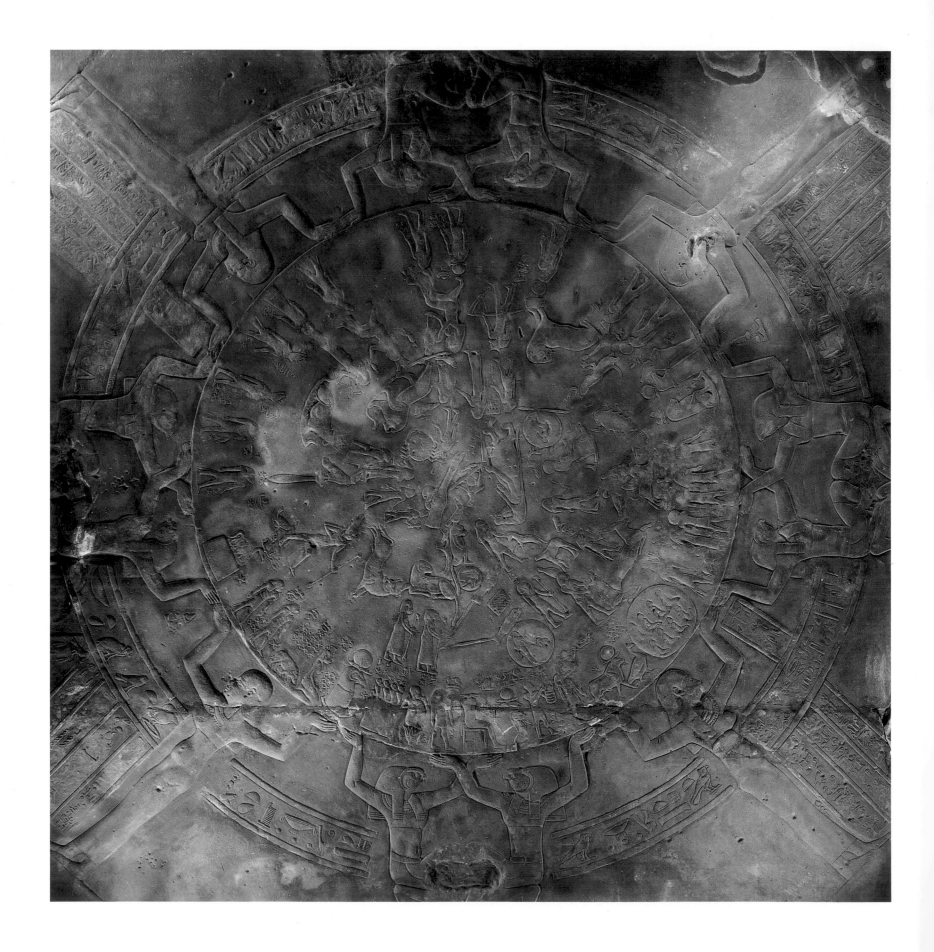

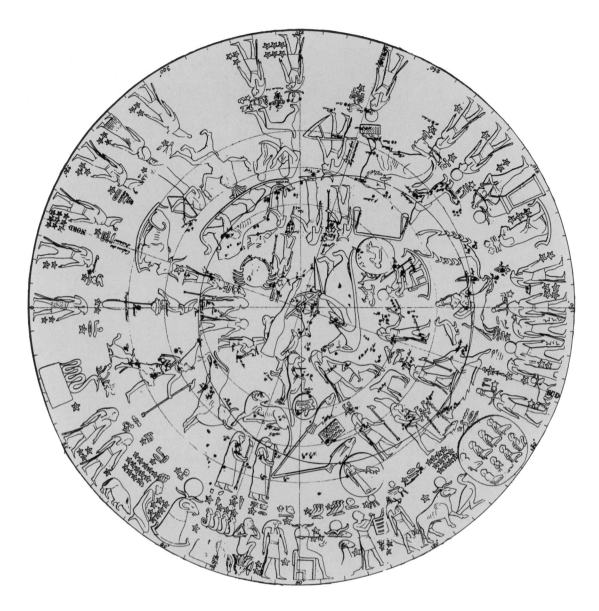

THE DENDERA ZODIAC. A sandstone carving of the first century BC, this is the oldest known representation of the Zodiac. The Babylonian constellations are combined in the central section with those native to Egypt, while around the edge 36 figures represent the Egyptian Decans.
The Louvre, Paris

THE DENDERA ZODIAC REDRAWN. All the twelve Zodiac signs can be clearly traced in clockwise sequence near the eccentric circle at the centre, although the positioning, for example of Cancer and Libra, is irregular.

The *Almagest* gives specific instructions on making a celestial globe, but no mention is made of two-dimensional star charts. In another work however, the *Planisphaerium*, he describes the polar stereographic projection which underlies the astrolabe: it is theoretically possible that the instrument was known to the Greeks of this period, although no material evidence has survived. Ptolemy warns that the problem of precession will in time render a star globe inaccurate, so he advises that the celestial equator and central meridian be not marked on the globe itself but on detached bands mounted around it, so that the globe itself can be rotated within the co-ordinate framework. This instruction was almost universally ignored by later Islamic and European globe-makers. The stars listed in Ptolemy's catalogue are given a number within each constellation: Aldebaran (not named of course) is number 14 of Taurus, 'the bright star of the Hyades, the reddish one of the southern eye'. Betelgeuse, brightest star in Orion, is 'the bright red star on the right shoulder'. To our eyes these textual descriptions could easily be replaced by graphic images, and it is hard to imagine that Ptolemy and his scribes were not motivated to draw constellation diagrams or maps; but if they were made in antiquity they have certainly not survived.

In the elaboration of cosmic models and the construction of the first star maps and globes, we see spherical geometry being used in the service of Greek analytical thought. The plotting of stellar positions on three-dimensional star spheres and the conceptual modelling of planetary systems were both evidence of the secular theoretical probing of natural laws so characteristic of Hellenic science. Yet alongside this rigorous intellectualism there flowed an altogether different, a darker, more equivocal stream of astronomical thought. For all the progress in precise observation and geometry, the metaphysical question still remained: What *were* the stars, and how did they relate to human life? If the cosmos was a closed, finite system, how did it cohere? What was the prime mover, and what was man's place in this flawless but mysterious mechanism? Behind the empirical pursuit of scientific knowledge, some minds would turn to the search for cause and meaning, the coherence beneath the observed phenomena. Plato had been in no doubt that 'the fixed stars are living beings, divine and eternal' and that the heavens are 'a moving image of eternity'. It was the elaboration of such beliefs that guided the astrological enterprise. When the universe was conceived as a complex of spheres and forces centred upon the earth, it became the aim of astrology to chart the balance of those forces at any given moment. Under the influence of Babylonian ideas, that moment became, classically, the moment of a person's birth, with the aim of revealing an underlying pattern which determined the nature and destiny of that individual's life. All the elements in this system — sun, moon, planets and constellations — could be disposed in an infinite variety of ways, and moreover they were believed to be linked to the earthly elements of air, fire, water and earth, and to animal and natural characteristics to create each individual soul. This interweaving of the human and cosmic material became articulated as the macrocosm-microcosm link, which became a ruling principle in the astrological enterprise. The key point to notice is that for astrology to develop into a credible science, it was dependent on precise observation of the celestial sphere, on precise zoning and charting of the heavens: it progressed on the basis of strict astronomical knowledge. Ptolemy himself wrote a seminal textbook of astrology, the *Tetrabiblos*, which summarizes a vast body of Hellenistic lore. Ptolemy is guarded on the question of the personality of the celestial bodies, and seems rather to teach that the influence of the stars and planets on human life stems entirely from the balance of physical forces in the universe. He elaborates this view by describing the meteorological effects that flow from the various conjunctions of planets and constellations, following the model of Eudoxus and Aratus. In the same way human life and human events are subject to physical influences from the heavens. The state of the heavens is seen as an objective moulding force shaping the human personality, obedient to laws which may be discerned but not ultimately explained. These concepts were later to become almost universally accepted in both Islamic and western astrology.

The Babylonian system of astrology, including the all-important Zodiac zoning, seems to have been transmitted to India, to Egypt and Greece itself by the fourth century BC, possibly as a result of the Persian conquest of the entire Old Babylonian region, producing the Achaemenid Empire bordering with India, Egypt and the Greek world. When in turn Alexander conquered this entire realm, the way was open for an unprecedented exchange of knowledge and beliefs in the fields of science and philosophy, and a complex syncretism of religion and magic. Not surprisingly, the precise sources, developments and interrelationships of these beliefs have not been fully worked out. But throughout the Hellenistic world, astrology became one of the acknowledged pathways of religious and intellectual search. It rested securely on astronomical skills and the astrologer was often, but not always, a scientist and philosopher too. It was in this period that the terms Chaldean and Magus testify to the eastern unity of astronomy and occult knowledge, and it is from this period that the earliest extant Zodiac survives,

SCORPIO AND OPHIUCHUS from a 15th-century manuscript of Aratus. We do not know whether classical manuscripts of Aratus and other astronomical works were illustrated or not, and we remain dependent on medieval reconstructions. This picture is typical of medieval constellation imagery, in which astrological interest focused attention on the qualities of the personified stars and planets.
The British Library, Add. MS 15819, f.9v

Typus Astronomie

CLAUDIUS PTOLEMY. Imaginary portraits like this appeared in numerous late medieval manuscripts and in early printed books. It shows the great astronomer with a quadrant, accompanied by a figure personifying astronomy. His crown represents a persistent confusion among medieval scholars that he was one of the Ptolemaic kings of Egypt. In fact, no scrap of information about Ptolemy's life, character or appearance has survived.
Gregor Reisch, 'Margarita Philosophica', 1512

the Zodiac from the Dendera Temple. Although this carving is from the Egypt of the first century BC it undoubtedly embodies Babylonian concepts and figures, married with the traditional figures of the Decans. For some reason divination by the Zodiac and by omens was regarded by the Greeks as native to Egypt, suggesting that Babylonian traditions reached Greece via Egypt. Herodotus described what was evidently a fairly mature astrological practice when he visited Egypt in 460BC:

'I pass to other inventions of the Egyptians. They assign each month and each day to some god: they can tell what fortune and what end and what disposition a man shall have according to the day of his birth. This has given material to Greeks who deal in poetry. They have made themselves more omens than all other nations together; when an omnious thing happens they take note of the outcome and write it down; and if something of a like kind happens again they think it will have a like result.'

Herodotus's tone implies a healthy scepticism, a reminder that at this date these mystical beliefs were novel and not readily comprehensible to many Greeks.

While empirical astronomy devoted itself to gathering objective data, astrology sprang from the subjective conviction of the organic unity of the heavenly and earthly worlds. One of the central and recurring beliefs in the ancient world that underpinned this search for unity was the doctrine that the original home of the human soul was in the stars. Pythagoras apparently taught that the soul fell to the earth and became housed in the body, and from this it followed that the object of man's spiritual striving is to liberate himself from this world and return to his celestial home. Plato echoed this doctrine, and it provided rich source-material for later astrologers who elaborated on the soul's fall through the many heavenly spheres, acquiring as it fell various characteristics — aggression from Mars, greed from Mercury, lust from Venus and so on. After death these qualities would be discarded as the soul retraced its path. To the Hellenistic and then the Roman mystery religions this vision of the descent of the soul was fundamental.

The mystery religions flourished for five or six centuries before the ascendancy of Christianity, and were undoubtedly a symptom of the quest for a mystical dimension to life denied by the formal state pantheon. The mystery rites themselves re-enacted the soul's progress through death and rebirth, the return to heaven. The Greek cosmological model was central to these religions and it became grafted onto various oriental cults such as those of Isis and Mithra. The Persian sun-god Mithra is usually portrayed sacrificing a bull, whose significance is uncertain, but whose blood and seed were the origin of life on earth. At the moment of sacrifice, the cloak of Mithra was metamorphosed into the sky, stars and planets, while the bull itself became the moon, suggesting echoes of ancient near eastern creation myths. In the Roman period the institutions and rites of Mithraism were undoubtedly interpreted in Neoplatonic terms, focusing on the ascent of the soul after death to the reign of the stars, many of these ideas having their source in Plato's *Timaeus*. Perhaps the height of oriental cult-influence in the west occured as late as the third century AD when the Syrian sun-god Sol came near to dominating the official Roman pantheon. Sanctuaries to Sol and the planetary gods proliferated throughout the Empire, and the Emperor Constantine wavered for a time between adopting Sol or Christ as the new deity of the Empire. The festival of Sol on December 24–25, the winter solstice, became associated with the mystery cults of dying and reborn gods, since after it the days lengthened as the sun regained its power.

Astronomy and cosmology lay close to the heart of Hellenistic and Roman religion, and the belief that human events are determined, or at least influenced, by the stars was universal. The pragmatic statesman Cicero thought it madness to deny that the stars and planets were personal deities, and in his *Dream of Scipio* he echoes Plato's vision of the soul being granted a glimpse of the cosmic spheres, a vision which re-appears in Dante in essentially the same Ptolemaic form. The problems of fate, determinism and free will thrown up by astrology were not lost on contemporaries. The prevalent secular philosophy of Stoicism taught a calm acceptance of the divine will, a life in conformity with the cosmic order, and the divine will in this context meant the pattern of man's fate that was legible in the stars. Part of the seductive power of the mystery religions was their offer of escape from this helpless determinism. A man who progressed through the mysteries could step out of the pre-determined path and shape his own destiny. The presiding deity of the mystery cult could unravel the decrees of fate and accelerate the adept's spiritual progress. In this relationship to the god there was thus a foreshadowing of Christian ideas of grace and salvation. The physical, cosmic framework of salvation was always the ascent of the soul to the heavens. The unswerving identification of the skies as the source, the guiding power, and resting place of the human soul was common to all cultures: it gave to the science of astronomy a distinct resonance, and to its practitioners the lure of supreme intellectual adventure.

2
ISLAMIC AND
MEDIEVAL ASTRONOMY

'Science has this much in common with magic, that
both rest on a faith in order as the underlying
principle of all things . . .'

— J. G. Frazer, *The Golden Bough*, 1890

H ic eſt ſtellaꝝ ordo utꝛoꝛuᵐ circuloꝛum
S eptentꝛiones duplices ad auſtrum
uertuntur. Figura aueꝛſis caudis in
uicem ſibi aduerſantes inter quas obliquus

B
Y THE SECOND CENTURY AD ASTRONOMICAL thought and practice had reached a historic plateau. The Greek sector of the Roman Empire produced no new figures of the stature of Hipparchus and Ptolemy, capable of advancing the observational or theoretical aspects of the science. The Romans' distaste for speculative science has often been commented on: new cosmological thought was beyond their reach, and, even on the more pragmatic level, they had enormous difficulty regulating their calendar. With the disintegration of Roman power, the preservation of Greek science in textual form, if not as a living tradition, fell to the scholars and scribes of Byzantium. The nascent Christian church was suspicious or hostile towards astronomy because of its identification with astrology. Astrology was one of the manifestations of paganism which the church set out to discredit. The mystery religions and the more philosophical forms of late paganism such as Neoplatonism were both dyed deep in astrological colours. Neoplatonism especially had at its heart the conviction that there were many levels of being, and that this world is a mere image of a higher archetype. There were many possible pathways to the higher realms of being, and the Platonic doctrine that the stars were divinities or intelligences among whom the human soul had its true home, meant that astronomy and astrology were seen as a science through which the chain of being, the harmony of human life with the cosmic order, could be studied and understood.

In some ways the Neoplatonic vision was attractive to Christian thinkers, but its openness to astrology was anathema to the orthodox early church fathers, whose faith was in a real personal God who acted in human history. Astrology appeared to them to dissolve God's power into vague cosmic forces, while the belief that the course of human life might be foretold from the stars apparently denied free will to man. The near-universal belief in astrology forced Augustine and the other theologians of the early church such as Origen to grapple with this problem of fatalism, and they arrived at a formula much repeated ever since, that the stars incline but do not compel: the pattern of the heavens indicate possibilities not certainties. The striking thing about such a compromise is that it does not seek to deny the basic validity of astrology: celestial influence was, in the ancient and medieval world, a universal belief among both pagans and Christians. It would remain possible for many Christian thinkers to defend astrology as one of the ways in which God's purpose may be studied and interpreted.

As far as our knowledge of it is concerned, the years 300–800AD represent something of a dark age of astronomy. The classical texts were all written in Greek, and the complete absence of astronomical tables in Latin meant that the serious practice of astronomy became nearly impossible. It is probable that Aratus's book on the constellations, *Phaenomena*, was known in Greek among eastern scholars and in Cicero's Latin translation in the west, and that copies of it may have been illustrated with rather crude pictures of the star groups. Aratus was certainly the best-known astronomical text from late Roman to early medieval times, distinctly non-specialist and non-technical. A second and similar Latin text was the first-century *Poetica Astronomica* attributed to Gaius Julius Hyginus, which was frequently copied and illustrated during the middle ages, and survived well into the era of printing. Hyginus was less concerned with astronomy than Aratus: he does not describe the appearance of the constellations, but recounts the legendary stories that lay behind them. Together, the illustrated Aratus-Hyginus texts formed the basis of all popular astronomy in the late classical and medieval period; they embodied a tradition that was rooted in poetry and mythology, while the Ptolemaic tradition had been far more scientific.

A few highly significant pieces of archaeological evidence survive from this obscure period. The ruined palace of Qusayr Amrah in east Jordan was built about the year 715AD

ARATUS'S MAP OF THE HEAVENS, from a fifteenth-century manuscript. The sky is seen projected from the north pole to a point south of the ecliptic — southern constellations such as Argo and Centaur are shown. It is debatable whether such images may be called maps, for they have no real precision. The concentric circles should be the polar circle, tropics and equator, but the positioning of the constellations is so imprecise that it seems the scribe did not truly understand what he was copying, and a number of mysterious figures have appeared which are not constellations at all.
The British Library, Add. MS 15819, f.3

for the ruling caliph, and although an Arab palace, its site had recently been conquered from the Byzantine Empire where classical influences still reigned. One of the rooms in the palace has a domed roof painted to represent the vault of heaven. Although in a poor state of preservation, a number of classical constellations are recognizable, centred around the north celestial pole, while lines evidently representing a simple type of locational system are visible. The constellation figures are drawn anti-clockwise, as if viewed from outside the starry sphere. This mirror image of what the observer on earth sees, is exactly the pattern found on the Farnese Atlas, and sources in classical literature are strongly suggested by the Qusayr Amrah dome. Less than two hundred miles from Qusayr Amrah, recent excavations at the city of Sepphoris, once the capital of Galilee, have revealed another remarkable link, this time between Roman and Jewish culture. After the destruction of the Jerusalem Temple in 70AD, Sepphoris became one of the most important cities of Judaism until the seventh century. The remains of a synagogue have been uncovered to reveal large intricate mosaics in which classical and Jewish subjects are combined. A large Zodiac naming the months and astrological signs in Hebrew has been found alongside depictions of the Ark of the Law and the Ten Commandments. The Sepphoris region was also conquered by Islamic forces in the seventh century, and these two sites thus form striking visual links between classical and Islamic astronomy. For the renewed pursuit of astronomical science and a renaissance in astrology took place not among the direct heirs of Greek and Roman thought, but within the dynamic new faith of Islam.

ISLAMIC ASTRONOMY   After the conquests with which Islam established itself, the eight and ninth centuries AD witnessed a precocious flowering of cultural activity. Having a source outside the great centres of classical culture, both the princes and theologians of the new faith sought to enrich their religion and their cultural life with the best elements drawn from secular science and scholarship. Centres such as the Abbasid court in Baghdad sought out texts and teachers of mathematics, philosophy, art and technology, culled from India, Persia, Egypt and Greece. The fundamentals of 'Islamic science' therefore were swiftly synthesized from many diverse sources, although it later acquired characteristics of its own, and the *lingua franca* of Arabic gave it a universality that reached from Spain to Persia. The works of Euclid, Aristotle and Ptolemy were all translated into Arabic by 850AD and underpinned their science and philosophy. Moreover there were specific motives which stimulated astronomy in particular, the most obvious being the need for an Islamic calendar, to be dated from the Hijrah of Muhammad (622AD). Then there was the need to calculate the times of prayer required by the faith, and to locate the sacred direction — the Qibla — of the shrine in Mecca. These two canons of time and direction engendered an elaborate study in the own right, and they were obviously dependent on precise observations, and on theoretical techniques of astronomy and geography. Medicine and human health too were regarded as closely connected with the aspects of the heavens, and every great figure had his physician.

One of the first manifestations of the new science was the appearance of a new type of table — the Zij — in which celestial times and positions of sun, moon, planets and stars were tabulated, with many of the mathematical aids for their calculation. In Ptolemaic astronomy, a complex geometry involving the sizes and periods of the planetary orbits had been described, and this had to be applied in order to calculate any given celestial position; in the zijes these positions were set out in tables for a given period of time. The availability of such tables was obviously a precondition for the widespread practice of astronomy. Many of the zijes were necessarily valid for one particular latitude only, and several hundred distinct families of zijes were produced in

ARATUS'S *PHENOMENA* in Cicero's Latin translation, from a tenth-century manuscript. Aratus and Hyginus were the popular sources of astronomical lore throughout the middle ages. Their close association with each other is strikingly embodied here in the use of Hyginus's stories to fill in the body of the constellation figures, while Cicero's texts appear beneath the pictures.

The British Library, Harley MS 647, f.4

centres from Toledo to Samarkand. The phenomenon of precession gave them a limited life, and they had to be regularly recalculated. Some were overtly intended as tools for casting horoscopes and other astrological uses. Later they were to be one of the vehicles by which Islamic skills reached the west as they were translated into Latin in the twelfth century, when they were influential in bringing Arabic numerals to Europe. Their method of construction was securely based on Ptolemy's *Almagest*; but if little that was both new and fundamentally important was added during these centuries, on a practical level the Islamic astronomers created the first recoverable phase in the history of genuine

ISLAMIC ASTROLABE, made in Egypt or Syria in 1235AD. An unusually fine brass and silver astrolabe in which the star pointers have been shaped into decorative forms of foliage, and, in the ecliptic circle, of some constellation figures. The lines of celestial latitude are clearly visible on the lower plate, and this astrolabe was provided with plates for the latitudes of Cairo and Baghdad.

British Museum, Department of Oriental Antiquities

star mapping. This took the form not of two-dimensional maps but of a remarkable series of instruments — astrolabes and celestial globes — which demonstrated a mastery of astronomical theory and practice far in advance of the science of Christian Europe.

The astrolabe was a hand-held instrument, mostly between six and twelve inches in diameter. It consisted essentially of two flat metal plates designed to be superimposed,

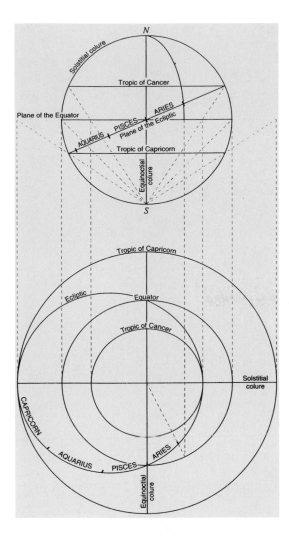

THE ASTROLABE POLAR PROJECTION derived from the celestial sphere. We are conceived to be at infinity above the north celestial pole, looking down on the starry sphere. The oblique circle of the ecliptic touches both tropics, and the tropic of Capricorn forms the limit of the projection.

the one above the other. The top plate was fretted into an open framework bearing a number of precisely-placed pointers. These pointers are really a map, giving the positions of several important stars, as if viewed from the north celestial pole. The starry sphere is envisaged as flat and outspread to a latitude below the celestial equator. The small instruments might locate only eight or ten stars, while the larger ones could show as many as fifty. This upper plate was called the 'rete', meaning simply a net. Tangent to the outer edge of the rete was a smaller eccentric circle which represented the ecliptic, on which the Zodiac constellations were marked. On the lower plate was incised a system of celestial co-ordinates, with lines of latitude and azimuth, and most importantly the horizon for the required latitude. When the rete was placed over this plate, the positions of a couple of prominent stars could be fixed, and the rest of the heavens could then be located. Of course the astrolabe was valid only for a given latitude, but it was not restricted to a particular time of the year, since the rotation of the rete over the horizon plate brought into view the stars of any given season. By separating the objective map of the entire northern heavens from the co-ordinate network which gave their actual positions in space and time, the astrolabe became an instrument both conceptually satisfying and immensely practical. It was equipped with sighting devices to determine the elevation of celestial bodies, and often had interchangeable base plates for different latitudes. When used in conjunction with Ptolemy's star catalogue, many hundreds of stars could be identified, and calculations of position, motion and time could be made. The rete was constructed — that is, the stars were plotted — by following an algorithm set out in a number of instructional texts on the astrolabe. The star co-ordinates are plotted in what is technically a polar stereographic projection, having the north celestial pole at the centre, with the celestial sphere down to the tropic of Capricorn outspread on a plane. The classical source of this procedure was Ptolemy's *Planisphaerium* text, and it is in effect a blueprint for a celestial map. Whether such two-dimensional maps were also drawn in manuscript is an open question: if they were, none have survived.

Although it was theoretically possible, it is not certain whether astrolabes were actually made in classical times. But also described by Ptolemy, and undoubtedly known and used by him, was the celestial globe, which was revived to great effect by Islamic astronomers. The globe as a conceptual model is much simpler to our eyes than the astrolabe, but it was more difficult to manufacture and far less portable. It was less practical too in the sense that what it showed was an abstraction which no human eye could ever see, while the astrolabe was geared to the observer's actual field of vision. The globe was not an observing instrument, and hence was not restricted in latitude nor, if correctly made, in time. The fact of precession gave the astrolabe an accurate life of 50–100 years at most.

One further instrument was less common but relates to the globe and the astrolabe, namely the armillary sphere, in which a small globe representing the earth is mounted at the centre of a series of metal bands which mark the celestial equator, ecliptic, tropics and polar circles. If sighting points were marked on the bands it could be used to measure celestial co-ordinates. If the starry sphere were added around the bands, clearly the armillary is transformed into a globe. Conversely if one can imagine the armillary to be perfectly flattened around the north pole, without distortion, the result is a northerly stereographical projection of the heavens, as used in the astrolabe. This perception lies behind the apocryphal story related by a thirteenth-century scholar that Ptolemy invented the astrolabe by accident: out riding one day and carrying a celestial globe, Ptolemy dropped it and his horse trod on it, the flattened instrument inspiring Ptolemy with the concept of the astrolabe. In the west the armillary was to become the recognized visual symbol of astronomy, and indeed of science in general, appearing in innumerable manuscripts and printed works, often in the hands of Urania, muse of astronomy.

RETE OF A TYPICAL ASTROLABE. The 18 pointers locate prominent stars in the northern sky, which is seen from above the central polar point. Approximately half of the sky is visible at any one time. The smaller inner circle represents the ecliptic.

The development of these sophisticated instruments was such that in the manuscript texts of all the important Islamic astronomers, no conventional two-dimensional maps appear: they were simply not needed. These same texts reveal the many levels of creative astronomical thought which flourished alongside the practical skills to which the instruments testify. Of the dozen or more great Islamic astronomers during the period 800–1200AD, none was more famous in the Christian west than Abu Mashar (787–886AD), known to Christendom as Albumazar. He was primarily an astrologer, and used sophisticated arguments drawn from Plato and Aristotle to deflect orthodox religious attacks on his art. In his *Book of Revolutions of the World-Years* and *Book of Conjunctions* he sought to demonstrate that human history, the rise and fall of principalities and powers, coincided with major conjunctions of the planets. Most sensational of all was his doctrine that the world had been created when the seven planets (that is the five classical planets, the sun and the moon) were in conjunction at the first degree of Aries, and that it would end when they all reached conjunction again in the last degree of Pisces. Fortunately unverifiable, this prophecy was widely brooded upon by astrologers of the middle ages, Muslim and Christian. Critical of the wilder speculations of Abu Mashar was the equally encyclopedic Al-Biruni (973–1048AD) who wrote extensively on astrology and cosmology, but who also explored in detail a variety of methods for projecting the celestial sphere into two-dimensional maps. This is puzzling since no such finished maps exist in any extant Islamic manuscripts. Although most of his writing was astrological in content, Al-Biruni's works, including one comparing calendars from different cultures, show an impeccable scientific basis. Yet in contrast with the more colourful Abu Mashar, his works were virtually unknown in Christendom.

The one Islamic astronomer whose fame rivalled that of Abu Mashar was Al-Sufi (903–986AD), whose *Book of the Fixed Stars* was illustrated with eloquent miniatures of the constellation figures which were widely imitated in Islamic astronomy, and which in turn influenced the iconography of early western star charts. Arabic astronomy from the pre-Islamic age had its own traditional images of the constellations, quite different from the classical figures: a giant human occupied both Orion and Gemini, and a water-jar or bucket covered Aquarius and Pegasus. Al-Sufi's work was based almost exclusively on Ptolemy's star catalogue, with the celestial longitudes augmented by twelve degrees to allow for precession to the year 964AD. The drawings show the principal stars graded into six different magnitudes symbolized by size. Not all astronomers were content simply to revise Ptolemy's listings to allow for precession. Original observation did form the basis for genuinely new catalogues, such as that of Ulugh Beg, made in Samarkand in 1437AD. Ulugh Beg was the grandson of the great Timur (Tamberlaine), and he built an observatory in Samarkand with monumental sighting instruments. These kinds of architectual instruments continued to be built in Islamic countries as late as the eighteenth century, while astrolabes and celestial globes remained in use virtually unchanged for 1,000 years down to the nineteenth century. Islamic science had a deeply conservative aspect, and the new southern constellations observed after the sixteenth century were never added to their maps of the celestial sphere.

In the field of cosmology, it cannot be said that there was a characteristic, orthodox Islamic view of the structure of the universe. There was within early Islam a strongly philosophical impulse which sought to provide a rational framework for faith, and this school embraced many Greek concepts. The Ptolemaic planetary system was widely known and became perhaps the accepted cosmology among Muslim scholars. Abu Mashar for example expounded the theory of astral influence as working through the physics of the Ptolemaic rings. But, as in medieval Christendom, there were several more mystical, even Gnostic, schools of theology, who claimed to discern the hidden or inner truths of the creation and the cosmic structure. The texts expounding these

doctrines were often accompanied by diagrams showing a plurality of human and cosmic elements. These diagrams share perhaps two main characteristics. First they unfailingly employ regular geometric shapes, especially circles, clearly echoing the Greek sense that the circle and the sphere are nature's most harmonious shapes. Sometimes the whole structure is a series of concentric circles, sometimes it is a group of adjacent or interlocking spheres. Secondly their motive is clearly to join intellectual and material categories in idealized relationships, to express an essential harmony that is invisible in the eye. In all these pictures, planets and Zodiac constellations are part of the hierarchy of being, and major figures such as Al-Biruni contributed to this tradition.

During the great period of Islamic astronomy, 900–1200AD, both observational techniques and theoretical mastery were in advance of those in Christian Europe. It was the translation of Arabic texts into Latin from *c.*1150 onwards which revived among western scholars the classical canons of scientific learning so long hidden from them. The Spain of the *reconquista* was the stage where this cultural exchange took place, and the most important individual was Gerard of Cremona, who worked in Toledo for almost half a century between 1140 and 1185AD translating Aristotle and Ptolemy, and whose version of the *Almagest* spread Ptolemaic astronomy throughout Europe, providing the text of the first printed edition of 1515. Equally important were the translations of the zijes and manuals the use of the astrolabe, which together placed in the hands of European astronomers the means to make their own observations and calculations. The most important tables were the 'Alfonsine Tables' promoted by King Alfonso the Wise of Leon and Castile and dated for the epoch of 1252, the eve of his coronation. They were disseminated throughout western Europe and helped to mould its astronomy for almost three centuries. By 1300 astrolabes were being made in Italy and France, and

ISLAMIC CELESTIAL GLOBE, made in Persia in 1275AD. Based on the star catalogue of Al-Sufi, this globe has over 1,000 stars, almost all in the northern hemisphere, inlaid in the form of silver points. The globe is centred on the ecliptic pole, and the oblique band is the celestial equator.
British Museum, Department of Oriental Antiquities

ISLAMIC CELESTIAL GLOBE REDRAWN.
Source: *British Museum Yearbook*, 1976

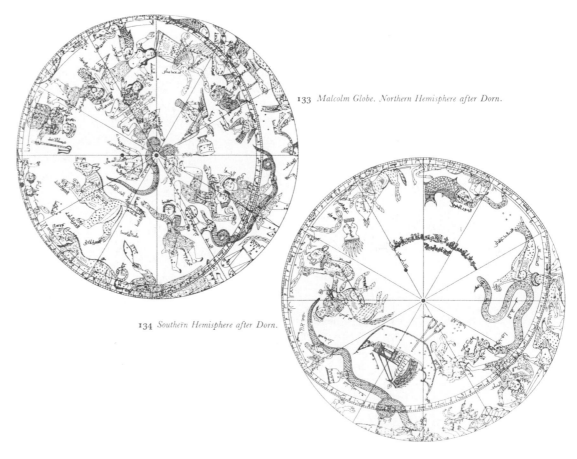

133 *Malcolm Globe. Northern Hemisphere after Dorn.*

134 *Southern Hemisphere after Dorn.*

treatises on its use appeared in the vernacular languages, including Chaucer's in 1391, written for his young son Lewis. One very specific legacy of Islamic astronomy was the naming of some 50 of the brightest stars. Greek sources had named only a handful of individual stars, such as Sirius — 'scorching', and Arcturus — 'bear-watcher', found in Homer and Hesiod. Most familiar star names, especially those beginning with 'Al-' (except Alcyone, which is Greek) are Arabic in origin: Algol, the 'demon' in Perseus, and Aldebaran, the 'follower' in Taurus. Many Arabic names were self-explanatory locations; for example, Mintaka in Orion means simply 'belt', Markab in Pegasus 'shoulder'.

ISLAMIC COSMOGRAPHICAL DIAGRAM *c*.1080AD. The universal intellect worships God in the Muslim formula *la ilahah illa'llah*, 'there is no God but Allah'. This formula has four words, seven syllables and in Arabic twelve letters. The Ismaili philosopher Nasir Khusraw considered that these corresponded to the structure of the cosmos: four elements, seven planets, and twelve zodiac signs. The intervening levels are modes of worship: purification, submission and glorification. This type of esoteric cosmographical diagram was highly valued in Islamic mystical philosophy.

SCIENCE IN THE CHRISTIAN WEST

The science of Christian Europe in the middle ages is the story of the encounter between conflicting intellectual authorities. It cannot be written in terms of empirical or theoretical advances, but in terms of the evolving intellectual motives that controlled and shaped it. The dominating and unifying force in Europe in the centuries after the dissolution of secular Roman power was of course the Christian church. Christian thinkers (like their Islamic counterparts) sought to construct a framework of information about the creation as a whole with which their central religious beliefs would be in harmony. Cosmology became central, since an understanding of the mechanics of the universe would lead to a knowledge of God. Medieval cosmology is not monolithic, indeed it showed enormous ingenuity, and the idea that nothing happened in cosmology between Ptolemy and Copernicus is vastly oversimplified. But what did remain constant was an approach to cosmology that was determined by *a priori* beliefs, so that intellectual energy was poured into elaborate speculations in which philosophy, mechanics and theology were held in balance. Empirical research and mathematical modelling were at a discount. The appeal which the closed, spherical universe had to the Greeks, had been the appeal of aesthetic geometry; to medieval Christian thinkers the appeal was theological, for all science was subservient to the religious motive. Questions concerning the structure of the cosmos, the shape of the world, the diversity of life, the origin of laws and society, were all seen as problems which related to the fact of God's incarnation in the world of man. Deprived of the rationalizing legacy of Greek thought, answers were sought in terms of *authority*; and the greatest authority of all was of course the Bible. Biblical texts which dealt with the divine ordering of the created world were examined and elevated into quasi-scientific dogma. Texts such as Job's 'Canst thou bind the sweet

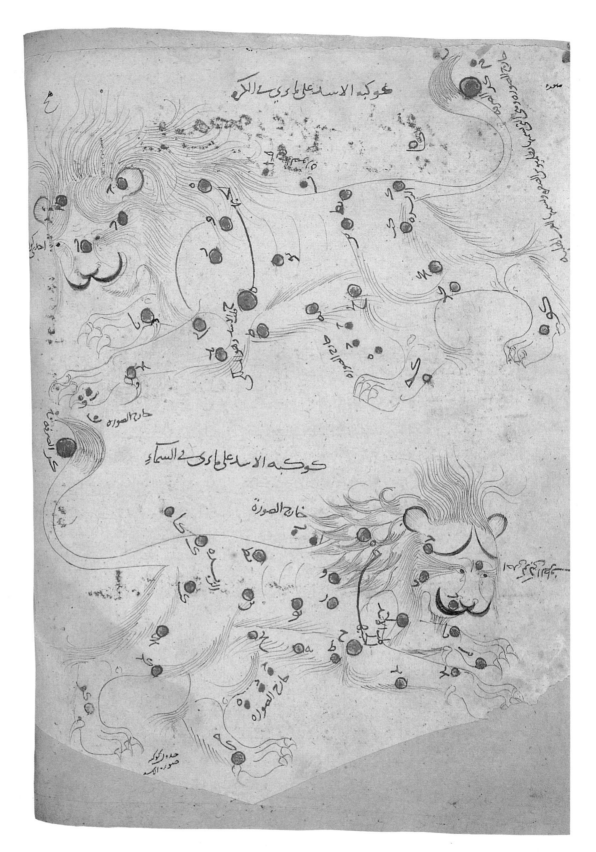

AL-SUFI, *Book of the Fixed Stars*, from a thirteenth-century manuscript. The work of Al-Sufi (10th century AD) was the most influential of all Islamic astronomical texts. Based closely on Ptolemy's *Almagest*, it catalogued and located more than 1,000 stars, and the manuscripts were habitually illustrated with pictures of each constellation, many shown in double aspect, as seen from the earth and seen on a globe.

British Library, O.I.O.C. Or. MS 5323, f.45v

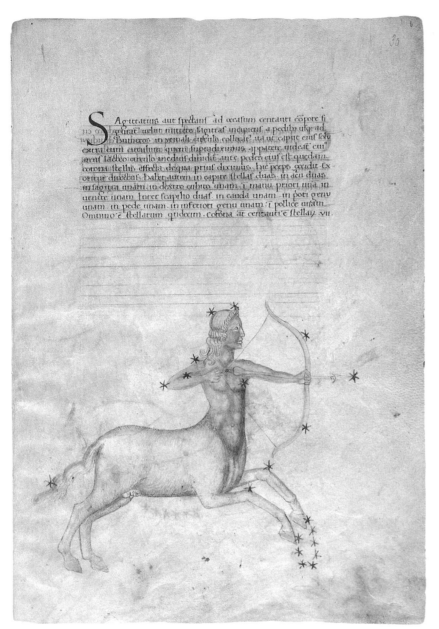

influences of Pleiades or loose the bands of Orion?' became the basis of an approach to cosmology that was neither rational nor empirical, but dogmatic.

Naturally it was recognized that the Bible had not pronounced on every conceivable subject, so recourse was made to secondary authorities, many of them late Roman authors such as Pliny, Martianus, Solinus and Macrobius, who offered encyclopedic but superficial collections of lore and opinion on philosophy, science and natural history. This form of literature was imitated by Christian encyclopaedists such as Isidore of Seville, whose works became in the middle ages an authoritative source on a whole spectrum of matters human and divine. In England, Bede wrote extensively on chronology and time-measurement, and in order to explain the basis of his thought in this area, he included an elementary treatise on astronomy, *De Signis Coeli*. In this milieu, science, philosophy and scholarship became overwhelmingly book-centred. The scholastic method of approaching any question was to ask: what have the authorities to say; how does Augustine, or Isidore or Bede treat this question? Neither reason nor experience

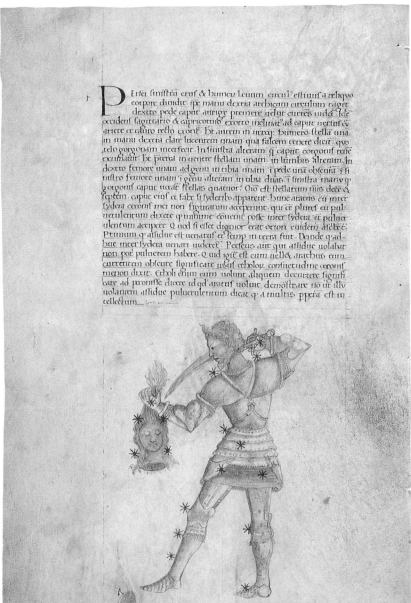

were considered capable of outweighing the authorities of the past.

But there came a time when the church, the custodian of all learning whether sacred or secular, was shaken by the introduction of a new authority to challenge the old, namely reason. In the twelfth century, Abelard, Albertus Magnus and above all St. Thomas Aquinas evolved a rational approach to such questions as substance, volition, motion and causality which was quite new in the tradition of Christian philosophy. The source of this new method was the rediscovery of Aristotle's works, newly translated from Arabic into Latin, in which reason and experience were employed to answer questions of physics, cosmology, psychology or ethics. To Aquinas, theology was a science just as much as physics was: it was rational knowledge of God derived from irreproachable sources, namely revelation and reason. The mystery of God was expressible in human language, just as the mysteries of physics were, and therefore subject to the rules and structures of logical thought. Nature, Aristotle's *physis*, has its necessary laws, and the task of reason is to create a science, *logos*, of those laws. The crisis over Aristotelianism

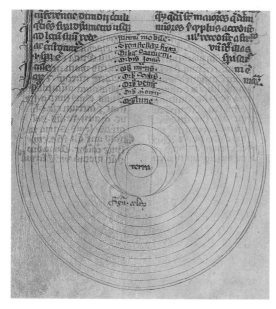

THE GEOCENTRIC UNIVERSE. The classical Ptolemaic structure of planetary spheres centred on the earth, from a 14th-century manuscript of Sacrobosco's *De Sphaera*.

Bodleian Library, Oxford, MS Ashmole 1522, f.25

BEDE'S CONSTELLATIONS. Bede's *De Signis Coeli* was a widely-used treatise of elementary astronomy, written to underpin Bede's work on calendar calculation. Although the work had a clear mathematical basis and purpose, its illustrations took the form not of geometric diagrams but of these vivid constellation images.

Bodleian Library, Oxford, MS Laud 644, f.8v

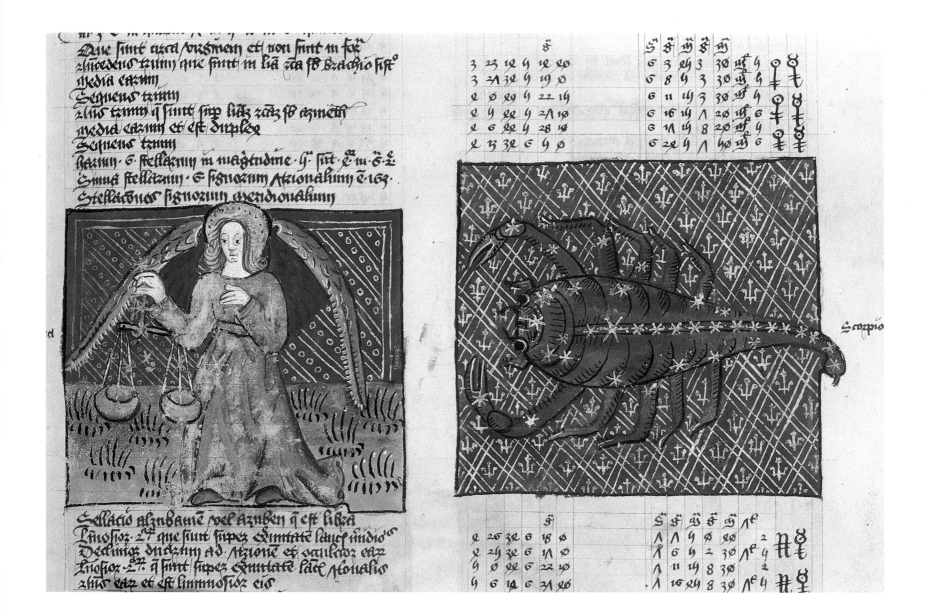

PTOLEMY'S STAR CATALOGUE, from a late Latin version of the *Almagest*, *c*.1490. A line of text locates each star within its constellation. Latitudes measured from the ecliptic are constant, but because of precession the writer of this text has given three longitudes: one for the time of Ptolemy, the first century AD; another for the time of Adam, set at 3496BC; the third for the mid-fifteenth century when this copy was made. The crude pictures contrast oddly with the precision of the mathematical data.

The British Library, Arundel MS 66, f.41

was not a doctrinal crisis, a question of new teaching about incarnation or redemption, but a crisis of authority thrown up by this new approach: were the teachings of Christianity true because the church guaranteed them, or because reason could approve them? Was the universe so because God willed it, or because it moved in obedience to rational laws of physics which even God could not alter, and which science claimed to discover?

Critical as this approach was for the church, it resulted directly in little new science, since the Nature that was lauded as the subject of rational science was in practice mediated through the theories and categories already devised by Aristotle. With the founding of the universities (Bologna, Paris and Oxford by the twelfth century; Cambridge, Padua and Rome by the thirteenth) the scholastic approach was, if anything, reinforced in the schools. Each discipline, mathematics, theology, law etc. required fundamental teaching texts which were of course culled from the 'authorities'. In this context the Bible retained its pre-eminence, with its innumerable commentators, while Aristotle became the new sophisticated authority to be weighed against the more traditional. This intellectual method clearly could not favour innovation in science.

Astronomy is essentially an observational and deductive science, while the scholasticism of the medieval schools was overwhelmingly non-empirical. A question concerning celestial bodies and their movements was answered not by looking, measuring and deducing, but by referring to Ptolemy and Aristotle. In the case of astronomy the most widely-used text was *De Sphaera* by an Oxford scholar who taught in Paris, John of Holywood, who took the Latin name Sacrobosco. Clear, brief and entirely derived from classical sources, from *c*.1230 onwards it provided an accessible statement of the rudiments of Ptolemaic cosmology. The mapping of the heavens in the graphic sense did not exist, since there were no models for the scholastic mind to elaborate. Many manuscripts of Sacrobosco's work were illustrated with small cosmic diagrams on the concentric-ring pattern. In the decorative art of the fourteenth and fifteenth centuries, it is interesting to see the vault of heaven filled with stars and having at its centre a circle or series of circles in which God is surrounded by the saints and angels. It was this cosmic structure which seemed to occupy the medieval mind rather than the relative locations of the stars. From the twelfth century there was a continuous awareness of Ptolemaic astronomy: manuscripts of the Latin *Almagest* were copied and circulated, complete with their co-ordinate tables and their workings in spherical geometry. Yet these two elements were never combined into maps or globes. Nor did occur to any scholars to transcribe into graphic form the northern star chart which they possessed in the rete of the astrolabe.

But alongside this inbuilt conservatism in western medieval science, there was a strong tendency towards the imaginative use of astronomy and cosmography. The ingenuity of the medieval mind, without which the great cathedrals could not have been built, produced some few technical advances of great importance, such as the mechanical clock, pioneered by Richard of Wallingford, Abbot of St Albans from 1327–1336. The clock provided philosophers with a satisfying new metaphorical image of nature, an image of a controlled mechanism which was to endure until the nineteenth century. The clock-face itself, which emerged in the fifteenth century, was clearly modelled on the face of the astrolabe, and its purpose was to symbolize the circular daily movement of the heavens through 360 degrees by the movement of the clock hands through 360 degrees. At the same time a number of instruments had been devised to assist in astronomical calculations: the torquetum, the equatorium, the albion — these were all circular analogues of the heavens, as the astrolabe and the clock-face were, and as such they might be considered to be related to maps. Richard of Wallingford wrote advanced treatises on mathematics, and the image of medieval science as entirely abstract is sharply contradicted by the work of such exceptional figures. Yet overwhelmingly the purpose of science and speculation was to understand nature as God's creation: all data and all theory must inevitably point to the end. For example, light was the subject of much study and speculation by Robert Grosseteste, Oxford's first chancellor, because it was considered on biblical authority to be the first creative principle, and a knowledge of its nature might lead to insights into the mind of God. Motion and causality were regarded as particularly important, for if everything that moves is moved, including the cosmos, all movement might be traced back to an ultimate source, which must be God.

This highly logical approach alarmed some churchmen, but its disciples attempted to disarm criticism with Aquinas's famous phrase that God was the author of 'the book of scripture and the book of nature'. Jean Buridan of the university of Paris meditated on the concept of impetus as a property which God imparted to the universe at its creation, as the clock is set in motion by its maker. Many contemporaries were apprehensive that such reasoning and speculation were fundamentally unorthodox, and in 1277 the church condemned a number of statements from the new rational theology. Some were abstract and hypothetical, for example that 'the first cause, God, could not make several worlds', because if he did they must be different from this, and this as

ASTRONOMERS USING ASTROLABES. From
a fourteenth-century manuscript.
The British Library, Add. MS 24189, f.15

god's creation must be perfect. This appeared to fly in the face of one of the basic tenets of Christianity, namely the omnipotence of God, and the fact that such speculations could acquire serious importance demonstrates the mutual interpenetration of science and theology. Yet medieval cosmology was far from monolithic, and even the fundamental Ptolemaic system was rejected by some. Averroës, the great Islamic philosopher, was an ardent Aristotelian, and could not accept the reality of the epicycles. According to Aristotle, circular orbital motion can only occur around a heavy body, and in space there are no heavy bodies: epicycles around nothing would be impossible. Averroës became widely known in the west and his doubts were carefully considered, but no alternative mathematical model to Ptolemy's could be found.

Yet the predominant motive of the new rationalists was not fragmentation but the search for harmony in nature and in thought. One of the strongest forces which served to crystalize the medieval aspiration towards order was the work of Dante. The author of the *Divine Comedy* had a complete command of contemporary philosophy and science, and his constant use of them directs the reader to his sources — this was true for his contemporaries and remains true for us. The very structure of Dante's hell and purgatory are formed from a series of concentric circles, progressing ever towards a pivotal or controlling point. This schema was clearly suggested by the classical insistence that the circle or sphere was nature's most perfect form, and echoes the Ptolemaic system. That Dante was well aware of this system emerges clearly in the *Paradiso*, which is full of explicitly astronomical ideas, indeed it is not too much to say that the central purpose of this final part of the poem is to offer a vision of the ordered harmony which God has built into the universe. Beatrice acts as his tutor to explain the moon's phases, eclipses, and the motions of the planets, and it is no accident that the figure who guides them in the sphere of the sun is the spirit of Aquinas himself. The miracle of Dante's freedom from earthly constraints, his journey through the spheres, echoes the deeply-felt belief that the soul's true home was among the stars. The vision of a journey through the cosmic spheres has sources in Plato and Cicero (and a later echo in Marlowe's *Doctor Faustus*). Perhaps the central mystery which Dante is exploring is how the mechanical universe can be moved by a spiritual force. Dante seems to have felt that Aristotle's philosophy did provide an answer to this metaphysical question through his definitions of matter and form. While matter was the material substance from which things are made, form was that which gave each thing its true quality. Form causes stars to shine and to move, while in man, form is the soul. Man is in fact a conjunction, a horizon between soul and body, while the cosmos was imbued by God with eternal harmonious motion, which expresses its form:

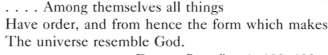

> . . . . Among themselves all things
> Have order, and from hence the form which makes
> The universe resemble God.
>
> Dante, *Paradiso*, 1, 100–102

On a very different level from Dante's grappling with metaphysical forms, other medieval writers made a more transparent use of astronomical symbolism. By Chaucer's time the astrolabe had arrived in western Europe along with much astrological lore translated from the Arabic. It has only recently been understood how extensively Chaucer's writings embody the spirit of the age by weaving astrological concepts into the structure of his plots. Built into the narrative of *Troilus and Criseyde* is a pattern of planetary conjunctions which counterpoint the rise and fall of human ambitions in love and war. Even more specific are some of the *Canterbury Tales* such as 'The Nun's Priest's Tale' which has an astrological subtext. The story concerns a farmyard cock, his wives and his narrow escape from a fox. These characters correspond to celestial bodies — the sun, the Pleiades and the Saturn respectively — and the story is related to four different arrangements of the heavens during the day of the drama. Since Chaucer was an expert on the use of the astrolabe, some scholars have suggested that he may have demonstrated this hidden meaning with the astrolabe after reading the poem. Later, after the advent of printing, paper astrolabes were commonly printed in astronomical books, to be cut out and mounted for practical use.

MEDIEVAL ASTRONOMER gazing at the stars. From a fifteenth-century French manuscript. The British Library, Harley MS 334, f.106

Chaucer died in 1400, on the eve of the new century in which celestial mapping finally emerged in Christian Europe, partly from Arabic sources, but also as a feature of the nascent scientific humanism associated with figures such as Nicholas of Cusa, Peuerbach and Regiomontanus. Cusa, a cardinal of the church, was a wide-ranging scholar some of whose speculations have led to his later reputation as a prophetic figure, even a precursor of Copernicus. Certainly he drew attention to the fact of relative motion, and suggested that it was possible that the earth could move as the other objects in the cosmos did. He took a keen interest in practical science, and collected many instruments, including the earliest known western celestial globe. Georg Peuerbach and Regiomontanus (real name Johann Müller, whose home town of Königsberg provided his Latin name) developed the study of astronomy in Vienna and later in Nürnberg, where they made a new epitomized version of Ptolemy's *Almagest* and new astronomical tables. These works achieved special fame for their authors as the first printed works on astronomy. The advent of the new medium meant that astronomical data and theories could reach a wider audience, and the simultaneous first printing of Ptolemy's work on terrestrial geography drew attention to the possibilities of using co-ordinate systems and map projections in the creation of maps on paper. Many editions of Ptolemy's *Geographia* contained the first scientifically-constructed maps ever seen in Europe, and it was only a matter of time before star charts constructed from the data in the *Almagest* would be drawn and printed. It was at this period too, *c.*1470–1520, that the great voyages of discovery first took European seamen far beyond the familiar waters of the Mediterranean. The problems of navigation this presented would not be solved with new terrestrial maps for a further century or more. But innovative mariners and technically-minded mathematicians were stimulated to devise new forms of instruments to facilitate navigation, and some form of two-dimensional star chart and three-dimensional star globe were basic requirements. Regiomontanus worked from 1467–71 in Hungary under the patronage of the humanist monarch Matthias I, among a circle of scholars which included Martin Bylica and Hans Dorn, who made and used the first celestial globe known to have been made in the west, a very fine instrument very much on the Islamic model.

ASTROLOGY

Knowledge of astrology in any detail had been virtually extinct in the west for many centuries until the process of translating classic Arabic treatises on the subject, such as Abu Mashar's, led to its revival. It is often said that in pre-scientific ages astrology and astronomy were the same thing. This is only true insofar as mature astrology is based

DANTE: *PARADISO*. From a 15th-century Italian manuscript. Beatrice explains to Dante that the universe is a hierarchy of being, all creatures obeying divine laws as far as they can perceive them. In the earthly 'sea of being' are creatures devoid of reason, while heaven is depicted as nine spheres ruled by the figure of love. *Paradiso* is full of ideas on astronomy and cosmology, on the physical and spiritual order within the universe.

The British Library, Yates Thompson MS 36, f.130

on the computation of celestial positions; therefore a knowledge of the rules and language of astronomy was essential. But it was perfectly possible for a late medieval scholar to study only the mathematical, physical side of astronomy, just as it was equally possible for the astrologer to devote himself exclusively to its mystical side, accepting his data from others. An example of the first school would be Nicholas Oresme (1320–82), the highly original French mathematician who likened the cosmos to the newly-invented mechanical clock, and who speculated on the possibility that the earth rotated in space. Yet he still spoke of the spheres being moved by intelligences and neither he nor any contemporaries sought to deny that the stars and planets do indeed influence human life. Yet such influence he thought was a question of nature, deriving from the qualities of those bodies, which might be studied and classified. On the other hand the attempt to predict the future, to manipulate fortune, savoured of magic: it compromised human freedom and should be shunned. The danger of fatalism was one that haunted many Christian and Islamic thinkers. Yet there were also secularly-minded thinkers who were impatient of the great tortuous labyrinth of astrology. Ibn Khaldun, the great

FRESCO OF HEAVEN by Benedetto Bembo *c.*1450. A typical medieval representation of the vault of heaven: against the background of stars concentric circles are focused on God. This embodies the classical doctrine of the perfection of spherical form, and the circles of angels are exactly as envisaged by Dante.
Civico Museo d'Arte Antica, Castello Sforzesco, Milan

fourteenth-century Arab historian, could write that 'Astrology is all guesswork and conjecture, based on the assumed existence of astral influence, and a resulting conditioning of the air'.

These were the views of an exceptional intellect, and they were undoubtedly running against the tide. The medieval conviction that hierarchical order permeated the cosmos led thinkers to seek and to find a whole series of links in the chain of being that bound man and nature together. One clear strand of thought identified this link as a system of physical influences, a theory whose classic expression is found in Ptolemy's *Tetrabiblos*. Ptolemy suggested that a power (*dynamis*) radiated through the ether, causing changes in all four earthly elements found in man, animals and plants. The moon for example affected human health because it caused a tidal flux in the body's humours. Given the keys to interpret these effects, a body of precise astrological knowledge, it should be possible to predict in advance both natural events and the course of human life. Albumazar had restated this theory of influence on a more spiritual level, proposing that the planets were deliberate dispensers of forces, that they were *intelligences*: since

THE MECHANISM OF THE UNIVERSE from a Flemish tapestry *c.*1450. The celestial sphere resembles an astrolabe, supported by the figure of Atlas and turned by an angel, under the gaze of God himself. Within the heavenly sphere many of the constellations are visible — Perseus, Pegasus etc. On the right the figure of philosophy is attended by those of mathematics and astrology, as well as Abraham and Virgil. The mixture of classical and religious motifs makes this an eloquent image of the richness of medieval thought.

Museo de Santa Cruz, Toledo

their effects could be rationalized, they must be rational. This belief was further strengthened by the observation that they were self-moving, unlike the fixed stars, and must therefore be possessed of purpose of volition. Much later, the more scientific Robert Grosseteste even spoke of the celestial influence falling on the earth like rays of light in complex geometric patterns, and that it was the variations in these patterns that affected human character and events. But if the planets were intelligences, how were they bound to their planetary bodies, and what was the nature of those bodies? It was to questions like these that the medieval intellect devoted much of its energy. Dante even speculated that ideas might pass to us from the stars. This universal belief in celestial influence implies a view of the celestial realm as an instrument, a mechanical force, through which God's power was mediated to shape human life.

This belief was elaborated in a vast body of accepted lore. Carnal man was linked to the animals, plants and minerals of this earth, and a knowledge of their properties

was essential to his bodily health. But his soul was linked to the higher levels of creation, the moon, stars and planets. One of each of the four earthly elements — earth, air, fire and water — dominated in each person and helped to determine his character. Each of the planets which might reign at the time of nativity produced characteristic types: Jovial, Martial, Saturnine etc. The Zodiac signs influenced both body and mind, and thus the science of medicine in the middle ages was deeply tinged with astrology. Not only individuals but professions, cities and nations had their stellar and planetary signs: for example thieves, shopkeepers (and later printers) were under Mercury, artists and musicians under Venus. Virgo was the star sign of Paris and Heidelberg, while Sagittarius ruled Cologne and Avignon. It is noticeable that while star charts are unknown at this period, emblematic figures of the separate constellations and planets appear prolifically in manuscript illustrations, modelled initially on those of Al-Sufi. There is an interesting

CHRISTIANITY AND ASTROLOGY combine in this 15th-century Book of Hours. God as creator is juxtaposed with Jupiter, his pagan equivalent, and with Aries, the first sign of the zodiacal year. The persistence of these pagan mythological emblems and themes throughout the Christian middle ages demonstrates the unshakable hold which astrology maintained on the popular mind.

The British Library, Add. MS 11866, ff2v–3

parallel here with terrestrial mapping: the medieval mappae mundi were not concerned to show precise locations, but the cities, the peoples and the natural marvels of the world were pictured in elaborate miniatures.

These levels of popular belief were vastly removed from the philosophical subtleties of Aquinas or Dante, but astrological emblems somehow flourished alongside the saints and the other Christian imagery. Judicial astrology was that branch of the art which sought to identify the most propitious moment for an enterprise — a marriage, a battle, a coronation. Thus political and courtly life provided the social setting in which, among coteries and intrigues, astrology flourished, and where the court astrologer was often the court doctor. The feverish climate of the fourteenth century — stirred by the Black Death, the Great Schism in the church, long wars between England and France, the radicalism of the Lollards, rumours of the Antichrist — all served to turn the mind to divination, and to seek in the stars the fate of the principalities and powers whose future appeared to be so troubled. Of course the actual predictions of the astrologer rarely came true, but far from weakening the art this had the effect of increasing the volume and complexity of astral lore. So deep-rooted was the belief in astral influence that remedies for man's defective knowledge and skill were sought ever more feverishly.

This heady marriage of astronomy and mystic science did not suddenly dissolve in the Renaissance period, which we see as the end of the middle ages, but it did become distinctly less Christian and more overtly pagan. The Renaissance largely reshaped European art, politics and religion, but not its science. Instead the sixteenth century witnessed a luxuriant growth of astrology as part of a fashionable cult of nature mysticism. Building upon the familiar Neoplatonic hierarchy of being, this important strand of Renaissance science sought to release and to master the hidden forces of nature through

PLANETARY INFLUENCE: a painting by Martin Schaffner, 1533. Each of the seven planets (including the sun and moon) sheds its own unique quality of light and its own influence. These were associated with seven arts, seven colours, seven days of the week, seven virtues and seven metals. The study and mastery of these correspondences was held to reveal the harmonies built into the universe. The eighth figure is the earthbound scholar.

Hessische Museum, Kassel

alchemy, occult wisdom and astrology. The archteypal Renaissance intellect was the magician-scientist Faust, and one of Faust's first concerns was to learn the secrets of the cosmic structure. Although not Christian, this was certainly not secular science either, for it was still serving the needs of a belief-system. In a curious phase of intellectual leapfrog, this neo-pagan science seized quickly upon the great breakthrough into the new scientific age, the Copernican Revolution. It has often been noticed that the rhetoric of Renaissance mysticism heralded in an uncanny fashion the sun-centred theory of Copernicus. Marsilio Ficino, a leading exponent of the Hermetic philosophy, could write:

> 'Therefore if you wish to see God, consider the Sun, consider the path of the moon, consider the order of the stars. Who is it that keeps this order? The Sun, the highest God among the gods of the heavens, to whom all the other celestial gods give way as to a king and a master . . .'

57

ZODIAC MAN from a fifteenth-century English manuscript. One of the central doctrines of astrology was that the parts of the human body were influenced by the twelve signs of the Zodiac — Aries ruled the head, Pisces the feet, etc. — and that the planets' presence within the star groups produced malign or beneficent effects. The movable dial, or volvelle, enabled the physician to calculate planetary positions and complete his diagnosis.
The British Library, Egerton MS 2572, f.50v–51

It is clear that certain implications of Copernican theory — the centrality of the sun, the worship of refining fire, and the newly-discovered vastness of the cosmos — suited Renaissance science perfectly, while orthodox religion retreated in fear. The fate of Giordano Bruno, burned in Rome for his blend of Copernican and occult beliefs, demonstrated the still indissoluble link between astronomy and the foundation of faith. It is a testimony to the weight of the intellectual superstructure that astronomy still carried, in contrast to the relative paucity of empirical practice. The reversal of that balance in the coming century was to revolutionize astronomy.

3
THE NEW SCIENCE

'Two things fill the mind with ever new and
increasing admiration and awe, the oftener and
more steadily they are reflected on: the starry
heavens above me and the moral law within me.'

— Kant, *Critique of Practical Reason*, 1788

THE STORY OF THE MAPPING OF THE HEAVENS cannot be written in terms of the history of cartography because, for the period so far covered by this book, *c.*3000BC–1500AD, cartography did not exist. It can only be written in terms of the history of astronomy. There were moments during the long era before the age of modern western science when celestial mapping might have emerged. One was with the work of Ptolemy (*c.*150AD) who designed, and probably made, a celestial globe. But he did not take the step of transferring that concept to two-dimensional maps. Intriguingly, this was also the case with his terrestrial mapping: he set out in detail a theoretical basis upon which to construct maps of the known world, but there is no evidence that he actually drew them. Another potential breakthrough lay in the hands of the Islamic astronomers of the tenth to the twelfth centuries who produced the astrolabe, but who once again did not take the step of transferring to paper the map which it contained. The sophistication and flexibility of the astrolabe meant that they had no reason to do so.

Throughout its history astronomy had its technical basis in mathematics, linear or geometric; but it was always being extended towards what was later termed natural philosophy — the search for the underlying causes and structures of nature. These causes were approached through the medium of religion, or astrology, or *a priori* logic, and the resulting philosophy produced a series of dominant ideas concerning the structure of the universe which shaped astronomy for most of its history: it was intimately linked with astral religion or theologically-based physics for many thousands of years in many different cultures. That celestial mapping did not emerge in any of these phases is more a matter of cultural and social context than fundamental intellectual obstacles. In none of the cultures in which astronomy flourished was there a tradition of scientific diagrams, or of visualizing philosophical concepts. The absence of a cartographic language is but one symptom of this. This situation changed emphatically in Renaissance Europe, where the natural world became the subject of visual interpretation in terms of perspective, mechanics, optics, dissection, and conceptual modelling. Celestial mapping only emerges in the sixteenth century, in parallel with the development of terrestrial mapping. Matters such as projections and co-ordinates had certainly formed part of Greek science, and were dealt with extensively by Ptolemy; but for all practical purposes these techniques were dormant during the middle ages, and re-emerge in the mid-fifteenth century in the context of the revival of Ptolemaic mapping. This coincided too with the age of printing and with the age of the new empirical astronomy associated with the invention of the telescope. The theories and discoveries of Copernicus, Tycho, Kepler and Galileo stimulated an intense and widespread interest in astronomy. It is no accident that calendar reform, overdue in Europe for many centuries, was finally enacted in the later sixteenth century. The Julian calendar year of 365.25 days was too long, and produced an error of 11 minutes per year. One thousand years after its introduction in the first century BC this had accumulated to seven days, and by the sixteenth century the vernal equinox, used to determine the date of Easter, had moved ten calendar days from its true date, a situation intolerable to churchmen and scientists. The complexities of the problem were great however, and of the many leading astronomers who were consulted, some (like Copernicus) refused to pronounce on the subject, and many years of thought, discussion and calculation were needed before the new calendar was instituted by Pope Gregory XIII in 1582.

In response to the new astronomical awareness of the late sixteenth century, the celestial map, as a conceptual model of the heavens that was easy to produce and to handle, was offered by map-publishers to an increasingly literate and scientifically-minded population. The structure of the star chart, the projection of a measured sphere, was dependent on the new language of cartography which appeared at the end of the

THE COPERNICAN SYSTEM from Cellarius, *Atlas Coelestis*, 1660. The most important event in man's evolving knowledge of the universe was Copernicus's discovery of the true structure of the solar system, published in his book *On the Revolutions of the Heavenly Spheres* of 1543. This later engraving dramatizes the centrality of the sun, and cleverly portrays the apparent cycle of the Zodiac through the daytime sky and the night sky.
The British Library, Maps C.6.c.2(2) p.30–1

COPERNICAN SYSTEM: the astronomer's own
diagram from the original manuscript.
(Facsimile.)
The British Library, X0622/170

fifteenth century. The key feature of that language, without which modern scientific
mapping could not emerge, was the co-ordinate structure, the ordered space imposed
by the grid of latitude and longitude, that was learned by Renaissance geographers from
the revived works of Ptolemy. The new art of 'cosmography', with its diagrams of the
earth and the heavens, became a characteristic Renaissance pursuit. With the growth of
map printing, all atlases from the later sixteenth century onwards included star charts of
the northern and southern heavens, often with diagrams of cosmic structures, the

Left: GALLUCCI ARMILLARY SPHERE, 1588. The sixteenth century saw an intense interest in scientific pictures and diagrams. Here the traditional outline armillary is given a naturalistic surface of five- and six-pointed stars, although the draftsman has not formed them into constellations.
The British Library, C.79.b.11

Right: TYCHO'S GLOBE, from a contemporary woodcut, 1598. Tycho used a large blank globe on which to plot his sightings of 1,000 stars. A wooden sphere faced with a thin brass skin calibrated to each minute of arc, it is no longer extant. The constellations in this picture have probably been added for decoration, and did not appear on the globe.
The British Library, Ac 9879/2, p.102

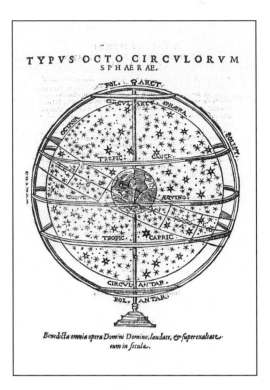

geometry of eclipses, lunar phases and so on. The star chart, a scientific document just as the world map is, became a publishing genre, subject to the intellectual and commercial demands of the day.

THE COPERNICAN REVOLUTION

The sixteenth century witnessed a quickening of scientific thought and the virtual rebirth of astronomy in its modern form, driven by a new approach to the problem of cosmic structure. The awakening of science came noticeably later than the revival of art, scholarship, discovery and commerce which we call the Renaissance, and when it did come in the mid-sixteenth century, the intellectual focus, as so often before in astronomy, was on the structure of the universe, the relation between the earth, sun, planets and stars. The Copernican Revolution in astronomy which placed the sun at the centre of the solar system has been widely seen as one of the great intellectual turning points in human history, causing a profound shift in man's understanding of the universe. With the perspective of history this is undoubtedly true, but it must be emphasized that this was no sudden cataclysm: the Copernican model won acceptance very slowly, and, a century after his theory was given to the world, serious astronomers could be found who rejected it entirely. The full implications of his revolution emerged only towards the end of the seventeenth century in the work of Newton, while the intervening century and a half had been a period of unease and uncertainty, hypothesis and experiment. It is well known that Copernicus himself hesitated for many years before placing his theories before the world, almost certainly because he foresaw the controversy they would cause. On the evidence of an essay which he circulated in manuscript, his ideas were essentially formed by 1510, while according to tradition a copy of his printed book *De Revolutionibus Orbium Coelestium* was placed in his hands on the very day of his death in 1543. There is no record that any one great insight or inspiration led Copernicus to his new theory. He was aware of the tradition that certain Greek thinkers such as Aristarchus of Samos (active *c*.300BC) had suggested that the observed movements of the

heavenly bodies might be explained simply by the motion of the earth itself, a motion that was however ruled to be impossible by Aristotelian physics. But having once seriously investigated this 'impossible' idea, Copernicus realized how elegantly a heliocentric theory explained the most puzzling type of planetary motion — the retrograde path. Between 1510 and 1540, he accumulated observational data and worked out detailed models of the paths of the planets around the sun. The result was a graceful, geometrically-satisfying system, but one which was powerless to explain the physics of such of a system: since it was clearly not fixed on a crystal sphere, how could the earth move? Copernicus's meditation on a sun-centred cosmos was not purely cerebral and geometrical. There is some evidence that, perhaps during his youthful studies in Italy, he had become aware of the Hermetic philosophy, in which fire and the sun were creative and purifying forces. This mystical language finds a strong echo in Copernicus's rhetorical description of the sun as 'the lamp in the temple', 'the soul of the world', and 'a visible god'.

Of the many profound implications that flowed from Copernicus's work, two of the most immediate were the size of the universe and the problem of falling bodies. First, if the earth were truly circling the sun at a radius which Copernicus calculated (wrongly) to be some 4.5 million miles, there should be quite clear stellar parallax: the stars on the starry sphere should move dramatically in relation to each other. Of course they did not, and the inescapable conclusion was that the stars were so distant that no parallax could be observed. While Copernicus did not overtly question the reality of the heavenly spheres — indeed he retains the word in his title — a universe of unsuspected vastness began to reveal itself. Secondly, classical and medieval physics affirmed with Aristotle that objects on earth fell in natural motion towards the still centre of the universe. But if the earth were neither still nor central in the universe, a new theory of weight and perhaps of motion was required. Copernicus's theory plainly raised far-reaching questions which in itself it could not answer, and some of his scientific contemporaries took refuge in the fiction that Copernicus had devised an abstract geometric model not intended to represent physical reality. A succession of outstanding astronomers set themselves the task of bridging the gulf between geometry and physics, a task in which empirical observation was seen to be crucial.

The first was Tycho Brahe, whose precise observations of the paths of comets across the solar system in the 1570s drove him to conclude that the crystal spheres were a myth. He also studied the appearance of a new star — a supernova — whose brief, striking and mysterious career in 1572–3 plainly challenged the classical doctrine that the celestial realms were unchanging and incorruptible. Tycho set new standards of observational thoroughness at his celebrated observatory Uraniborg ('Castle of the Heavens') on the Danish island of Hven, yet he was one of those who could not reconcile himself to the Copernican system. A moving earth was an absurdity to him, and he devised a compromise theory in which the five planets did orbit the sun, while the sun still circled the earth. This required the paths of planets to cross each other, which would have been impossible in the presence of the celestial spheres. This theory was published in 1588 and it attracted much support because it confirmed the evidence of our senses that the earth does not move, and because it re-enthroned man at the centre of the

TYCHO'S PLANETARY SYSTEM (1588) from Cellarius's *Atlas Coelestis*, 1660. Tycho was one of a number of astronomers who could not accept that the earth was moving in space. Yet his observations convinced him that the planets did revolve around the sun. He devised his own theory in which the planets orbited the sun, while the sun in turn orbited the earth. The earth was thus restored to the centre of the cosmos.
The British Library, Maps C.6.c.2

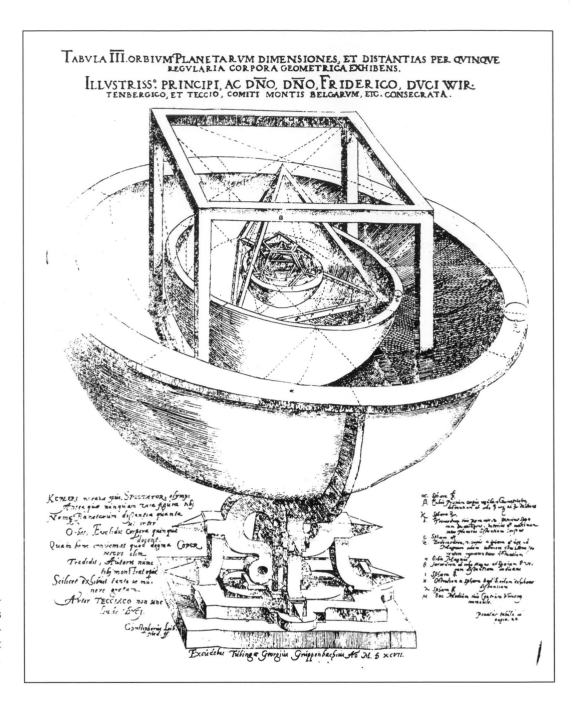

KEPLER'S PLANETARY MODEL, from *Mysterium Cosmographicum*, 1596. The regular solids whose proportions Kepler conceived to determine the orbits of the planets. One of the most sophisticated cosmic diagrams ever published. The British Library, C.54.bb.34

universe. Tycho constructed a large, elaborate celestial globe which must be counted one of the most important in the history of astronomy. It has not survived, but he left a description of it in his book on astronomical instruments published in 1598. It was one and a half metres in diameter, formed of wood covered with thin brass sheets on which were etched the ecliptic, the equator and a meridian. The calibration was of unmatched precision, with each minute of arc being engraved. As his observation and cataloguing proceeded, Tycho marked each star on this globe, so that by 1595 it displayed the locations of 1,000 stars. It is easy to use the phrase 'new star catalogue', but this accurate positioning of hundreds of individual stars depends on the meticulous measurement on an invisible co-ordinate system of a few fundamental stars to which the others may then be related. Tycho laboured for years to secure instruments of unprecedented accuracy:

they were all pre-telescopic of course, and consisted of various large sighting devices such as the famous mural quadrant and the huge armillary. Tycho's was a radical commitment to a new type of empirical astronomy: if the astronomer wished to understand the heavens he must observe and measure them, he must see them as they are, not theorize or be enslaved by dogma. The fact that Tycho produced no star maps perhaps tells us something of their limited role. His star catalogue was for the committed professional astronomer who would use it with his own instruments to observe the stars. A map was a demonstrational aid which the non-specialist without instruments might use to identify what he saw in the sky. The distinction is an important one, for it explains

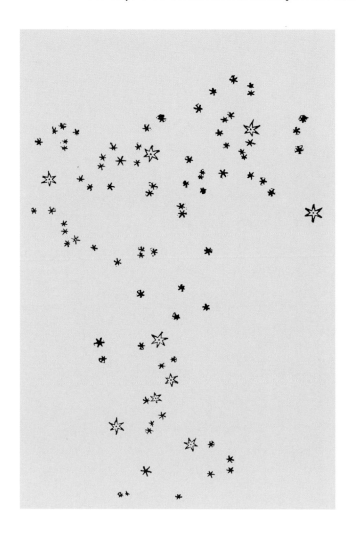

GALILEO: Map of stars in Orion's belt and sword. The first star map made with the aid of a telescope: Galileo found some 80 stars, where the naked eye sees perhaps a dozen.
The British Library, C.112.c.3

why the star chart became the province of the commercial map publisher, while for the serious astronomer it was the star catalogue which mattered.

The astronomer whose achievement was to bridge the gulf between theoretical geometry and physical motion was Johannes Kepler. Working within the Copernican framework, from his earliest career his thought tended to the philosophical, to the quest for ultimate causes in the universe. He was a creative astrologer, committed to the search for the links and harmonious relationships among the many realms of nature, including man. He was convinced that the soul received at birth the imprint of the reigning celestial pattern, and he pondered the possible mechanisms by which this might operate. For a time he considered that the quality of light radiating from each celestial body might vary, and that light could therefore be the medium of cosmic force. He also explored

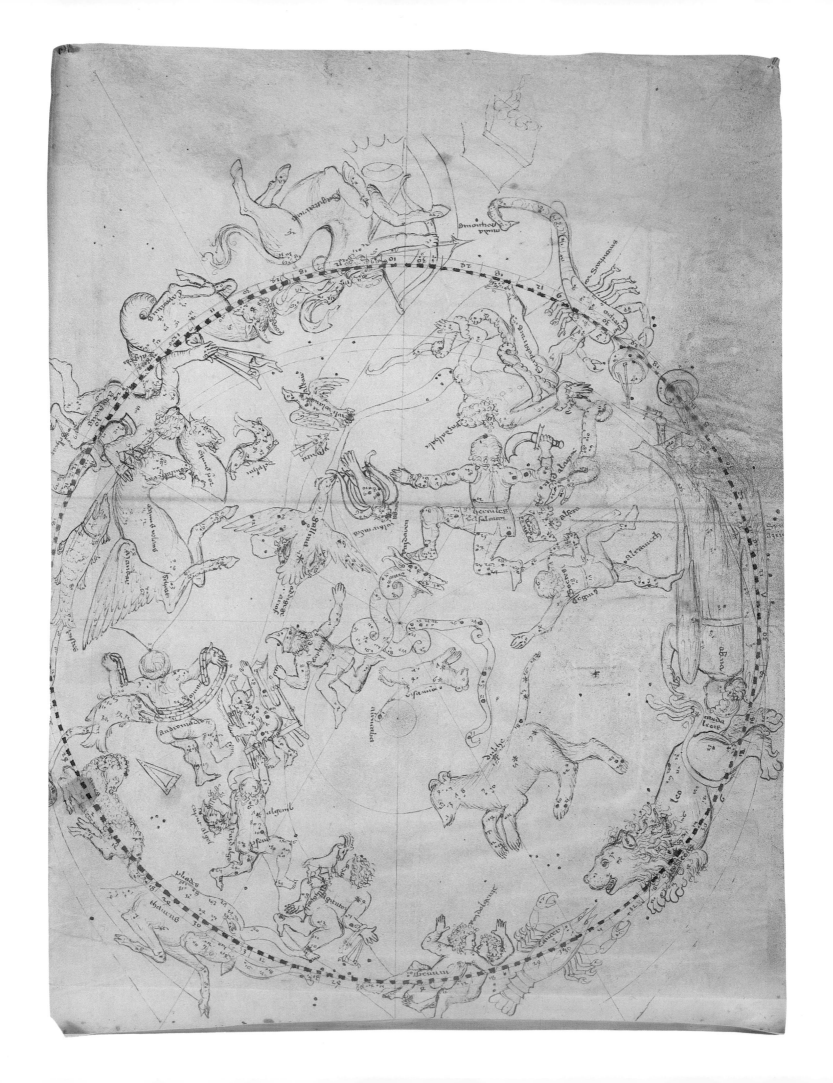

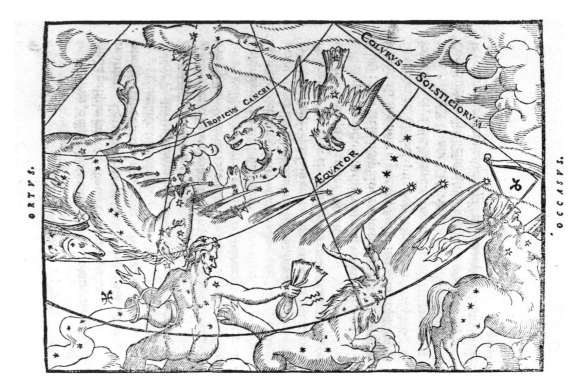

THE GREAT COMET OF 1577. The comet, which was so important to Tycho, is shown progressing from Sagittarius to Pegasus during November and December of that year. Numerous broadsheet pictures of comets were printed in the sixteenth and seventeenth centuries, many of them crude and sensational; this one is much more precise and scientific. Comets were of great concern during this period because they helped to overturn the traditional view of the enclosed, stable, unchanging cosmos.

Royal Observatory, Edinburgh

THE VIENNA MANUSCRIPT *c.*1440. The earliest surviving genuine star map of the northern heavens, plotted within co-ordinates and projected from the ecliptic pole. The stars are marked with the numbers in Ptolemy's star catalogue. The origin of this map is unknown, but it became the pattern for all future star charts. Manuscript maps like this were probably circulating among Renaissance scientists many years before a printed version appeared.

Oesterreichische Nationalbibliothek, Vienna

the correspondences between celestial configurations and meteorology, in the tradition of Ptolemy's *Tetrabiblos*. One of his most famous attempts to lay bare the secret harmony of the universe was his geometric model of the solar system. Apparently he discovered in a flash of inspiration that the ratios of the planetary orbits conformed to a series of regular solids: between Saturn and Jupiter the cube, between Jupiter and Mars the tetrahedron, between Mars and Earth the dodecahedron, between Earth and Venus the icosahedron, and between Venus and Mercury the octahedron. These are the five regular solids of classical geometry; there are no others. This intriguing model does indeed approximate to the truth, but it transpires to be an isolated relationship, unrelated to any laws of science. Kepler saw it as confirming his sense of cosmic harmony, and he continued his researches into the planetary paths. Between 1609 and 1619 he published what became known as his three laws of planetary motion: that the orbits of the planets are not circles but ellipses with the sun at one focus; that their radius vectors sweep out equal areas in equal time, hence in the elliptical orbits their velocities cannot be constant; and that their orbital period is in direct mathematical relationship to their solar distance, that is, the cube of the distance is in constant ratio to the square of the time (e.g. Jupiter is 5.2 astronomical units from the sun; 5.2 cubed is 140.6, and the square root of 140.6 is 11.9, which is Jupiter's orbital period in earth years). The significance of these discoveries was immense for they signalled the approaching end of *a priori* Aristotelian physics, making possible their replacment by empirically-derived laws of mechanics. Abstract doctrines such as the necessity of pure, spherical motion, were banished, as was the complex network of epicycles, which had survived both Copernicus and Tycho. Kepler had not perhaps discovered the underlying cosmic harmony which he sought, but his dynamic model was an account of physical reality, not an elegant hypothesis. Yet the motive power of the model, the forces which held the universe in equilibrium, remained as mysterious as ever.

The seal was set on this remarkable period of astronomical innovation by the discoveries of Galileo. Less profound as a theorist than Copernicus or Kepler, Galileo used the newly-invented telescope to look with critical eyes at the solar system, and he

Opposite: DÜRER'S STAR CHARTS, 1515. The first printed star charts, they bear an unmistakable resemblance to the Vienna manuscript. The constellations are portrayed in rear-view and proceed anti-clockwise around the ecliptic, in the classical fashion. The portraits of Ptolemy, Aratus, Al-Sufi and Manilius proclaim the intellectual descent of these charts, which were seminal for all future celestial maps.

rigorously interpreted what he saw. When he trained his telescope on any region of the sky, apparently empty space was resolved into previously unseen star-fields. He illustrated this by publishing a new map of part of the constellation Orion, showing some eighty stars, where the naked eye could detect no more than a dozen. The concept of scale cannot be precisely applied to celestial maps, but Galileo's achievement here may be thought of as the equivalent of producing the first large-scale map of one of the constellations. None of his discoveries was more significant than that of the moons of Jupiter, announced in his famous book *Sidereus Nuncius* ('The Starry Messenger') of 1610. Here was a system of celestial master and satellite exactly mirroring the supposedly unique relationship of the sun and its planets. Clearly there were multiple centres of motion in the solar system, and therefore laws of motion which were valid throughout the universe: this discovery now undermined man's former view of the uniqueness and centrality of the earth.

Contemporary with Galileo, one of the foremost philosophical minds of the age turned his attention to the baffling problems of cosmic mechanics thrown up by the new science. René Descartes proposed to replace the celestial spheres by vortices of invisible, subtle matter which carried the earth and the heavenly bodies in their paths. It was as ingenious as it was unverifiable, and the wide support it attracted throughout the seventeenth century shows clearly the extreme difficulty that scientists and philosophers had in conceiving of a physical mechanism that could hold the universe together: the concept of empty space was unthinkable. The addiction to the idea of direct physical cohesion that lay behind the classical notion of the spheres, and behind the Cartesian vortices, was finally vanquished by the genius of Isaac Newton. His statement of the laws of gravity, velocity and mass broke through the psychological barriers of his time to the discovery of action at a distance, of force acting through empty space, so inconceivable to his predecessors. Newton's theory was worked out with austere mathematical purity, and it is typical of the quality of his mind that, in this great age of scientific images, he alone had no resort to visual diagrams or conceptual models. Newton's dynamic theory of cosmic structure was to satisfy the scientific mind for two centuries and more, and it marked the final separation of astronomy from astrology: by the later seventeenth century the universe was no longer seen as a closed system of spheres where astral forces radiated upon the earth. In removing the earth from the centre of the cosmos, science had shattered the classical model upon which astrology had been built, and Newton's dynamics rationalized the entire cosmic structure. Astrology was based on a certain physical perspective on the earth and the heavens, and the expanding universe of the sixteenth and seventeenth centuries first shifted, then destroyed, that perspective. Newton's work was the final vindication of empirical, mathematical astronomy, against the scholastic authorites of the past; significantly the youthful Newton inscribed in one of his notebooks 'Amicus Plato, amicus Aristoteles, magis amica veritas' — 'Plato is my friend, Aristotle is my friend, but my greatest friend is truth'.

THE EARLIEST MODERN STAR CHARTS

It was in this period of revolutionary astronomical change that the star chart established itself as a scientific reference document comparable to the world map. The Copernican revolution and the problems it threw up, re-focused attention on every aspect of the heavens, and it demanded new data and new methods of observation, study and interpretation. This was the empirical revolution in astronomy, and its effect was to produce an outpouring of research and of popular publications which described and portrayed the skies. The emergence and proliferation of published star maps after 1600 would have been unthinkable without the impetus provided by the central problem of

planetary physics. The paths of the planets were not of course directly shown on published star charts, for the chart would then be valid only for a period of months. Planetary positions were published in tables known as ephemerides, which the observer, professional or amateur, astronomer or astrologer, could then relate to his star chart. By the early seventeenth century there was a conscious sense that this was a new age of astronomy, and that its leading figures rivalled the classical founders of the science. The initial problem of designing a conceptual model of the starry sphere, a stellar reference system, was solved long before the problem of cosmic structure. The radical remodelling of the world map which accompanied the revival of classical geography had a crucial influence on the emergence of the star chart: the appearance in Europe of a fully-fledged map of the heavens was exactly contemporary with the earliest classically-modelled, co-ordinated world maps. Individual constellation figures, some more, some less, scientific in style, had remained familiar throughout the middle ages, yet the most authoritative astronomical text, Ptolemy's *Almagest*, was not traditionally illustrated (except with

Right: HONTER'S STAR CHARTS, 1541. Although stylistically reminiscent of the Dürer planispheres, on these charts the constellations are seen as from the earth, proceeding clockwise around the ecliptic. Honter has also shown the Zodiac bounding both hemispheres, and his human figures are drawn in a vernacular style, clothed as northern Europeans of the sixteenth century.
The British Library, Maps C.1.c.2(2)

Left: APIAN'S STAR CHART from *Astronomicon Caesareum*, 1540. Obviously derived from Dürer's planispheres, the novelty of Apian's map is its combination of the northern and southern spheres into one chart: the projection from the pole is extended south beyond the ecliptic, so that the south pole would eventually become a line encircling the whole map. In this way all 48 classical constellations can be shown. The lateral distortion becomes extreme, as can be seen from the length of the ship Argo. Nevertheless it is surprising that this ingenious form of star map was not more widely imitated.
The British Library, Maps C.6.d.5

IMAGINES CONSTELLATIONVM
BOREALIVM.

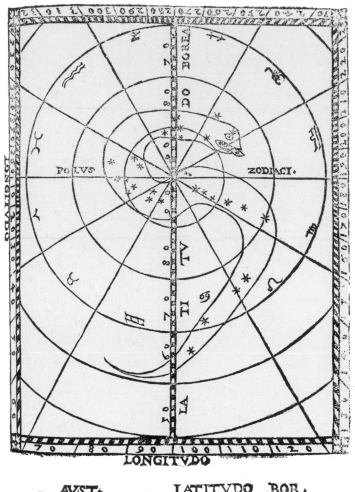

geometric figures) and before the early sixteenth century no great interest had been shown in diagrams which located the stars and constellations on the vault of the heavens.

The earliest known genuine star map is essentially a new creation dating from *c.*1440, the unique Vienna manuscript. It appears in an anonymous astronomical work *De Composicione Sphere Solide*, and it forms the prototype of an image that was to be replicated and elaborated hundreds of times over the next three centuries. The 48 Ptolemaic constellations are shown, with the stars numbered according to the catalogue in the *Almagest*. The maps are projected from the ecliptic poles, so that the ecliptic itself, adorned with the Zodiac figures, forms the maps' edge. The Milky Way is shown, and the 360 degrees of the ecliptic circle are individually marked, subdivided into blocks of

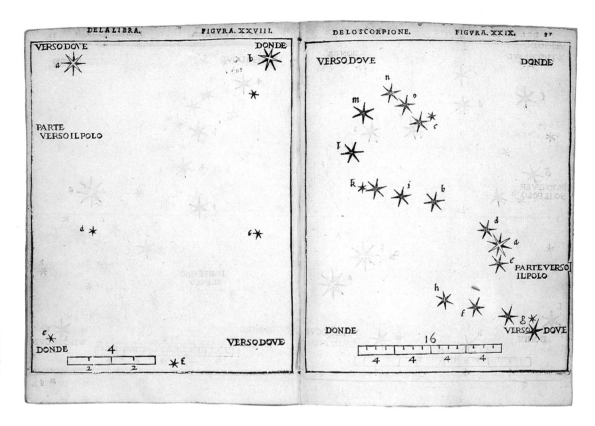

PICCOLOMINI: Scorpio, from *De le Stelle Fisse*, 1540. Piccolomini's book was the first printed celestial atlas and it was highly detailed. But its austere style, lacking co-ordinates and the constellation figures, limited its popularity.
The British Library, 530.d.8

GALLUCCI's *Theatrum Mundi*, 1588. An early woodcut star atlas illustrating each of the constellation figures, with a catalogue of their stars. Gallucci followed the star catalogue of Copernicus rather than Ptolemy. In order to avoid the changes caused by precession, Copernicus measured celestial longitude not from the vernal equinox, which is itself a slowly-moving point, but from the first star in Aries. Thus the movement of the entire celestial sphere leaves all co-ordinates constant in relation to each other. Gallucci has used a trapezoid frame to indicate that these maps are sections of the celestial sphere, narrowing towards the poles.
The British Library, 779.b.11

30 degrees, one block for each Zodiac sign. There is no bar of altitude or celestial latitude. The source, origin and purpose of this, the oldest two-dimensional star map, are all unknown. The scholar who drew it (or if it is a copy, the scholar who drew the original) had made the crucial transition from globe to map, and the lack of an altitude scale is suggestive: while Islamic globes always bore the ecliptic or equatorial degrees on their surface, the latitude degrees were almost always marked on a detached meridian. A certain Islamic influence is detectable in the iconography of some constellations, for example the scimitar in Hercules's hand, and the turban-style crown or helmet worn by Cepheus. It seems virtually certain that the unknown author of this planisphere did what had been inherently possible for many centuries, but which no one had felt impelled to do: working from a celestial globe, and perhaps from an astrolabe too, both probably Islamic, he spread out the starry sphere to form the first paper star chart, and created a conceptual model of the heavens which man would never see, but which would become permanent in western science. It may truly be described as a map and not a picture,

because its co-ordinate framework gives it a measured structure in which each part of the map is precisely related to the other and to reality.

The context and purpose of the Dürer planispheres are not known with any certainty, but it is clear that they were the printed culmination of half a century of thought and experiment among a group of intellectuals centred on Vienna and Nürnberg. The unknown author of the Vienna manuscript must have been involved in this process at any early stage, and Martin Bylica of Cracow University was another associate: he commissioned from the instrument-maker Hans Dorn the first European star globe, cast in metal, very much on the Islamic model and strikingly similar to the Vienna manuscript. The key figure was Regiomontanus, whose influential epitome of the *Almagest* was completed in 1463 but not published until 1496. After studying in Vienna he was lecturing on Islamic astronomy in Padua during the 1460s. He then travelled to Hungary and worked with Martin Bylica, before settling in Nürnberg in 1471, where he taught and published. It is known that he and Bylica were very familiar with Islamic globes and astrolabes, and it seems certain that manuscript star charts were circulating among these scholars. The moment had plainly arrived when spherical geometry, Ptolemaic co-ordinates and the visual example of Islamic instruments should all combine to produce the two-dimensional planispheric star map. The first printed examples were designed as woodcuts by Dürer and printed in Nürnberg in 1515, and were immensely influential in shaping the genre of the printed star chart over the following three centuries.

The cartouche at the foot of the southern chart explains that two Nürnberg mathematicians, Johann Stabius and Conrad Heinfogel, plotted the star positions on the charts, while Dürer was responsible for the artistic design. An important point relating to this and all subsequent star maps is the distinction between the map itself and the star catalogue on which it was based. The materials of the Dürer star charts are thoroughly Ptolemaic: the constellations are the 48 listed in the *Almagest*, and the stars are identified by the numbers which Ptolemy gave them. The altitude of stars north or south of the ecliptic is unchanging, but the phenomenon of precession means that all celestial longitudes will shift westwards by one degree every 72 years. If Stabius and Heinfogel had used Ptolemy's co-ordinates from 150AD all the Zodiac constellations would have been nineteen degrees out of position. The Alfonsine tables of 1252AD had updated Ptolemy, and the Nürnberg group further corrected those figures to allow for precession since that date. It would be open to any artist or publisher simply to copy the form of a celestial map from any available model, but if the aim was to produce a scientific document for the discerning reader, then up-to-date longitudinal positioning of the stars was essential. Dürer and his scientific editors were plainly aware of the classical tradition that the constellation figures should be portrayed as if seen from the outside of the starry sphere: the images are seen in rear-view and progress anti-clockwise around the heavens. Dürer has to some extent westernized his images, for example Hercules now bears a club and a lion skin. In the striking marginal portraits Dürer acknowledges the sources and authorities of all astronomical works: Ptolemy, Aratus, Al-Sufi (his name latinized to Azophi) and Marcus Manilius. The last is the least familiar: a minor Roman poet who wrote on astrology, and whom Dürer happened to know because the first printed edition of his works had been issued in Nürnberg some years earlier.

The Dürer planispheres represent both a beginning and an end. They inaugurated a genre of publishing in which a scientific document sought to give delight through its artistry, a genre which was to flourish for 300 years. But it also forms the culminating link in an intellectual chain whose length is deeply impressive. Constellation figures traceable in some cases to Mesopotamia in the second millenium BC, were placed within a geometric framework by Greek science, a framework perpetuated by Islamic scholars

SCHÖNER'S CELESTIAL GLOBE, *c.*1533. The first printed celestial globe. Johann Schöner was the most influential early globe-maker, establishing Nürnberg as the European centre of the craft, and setting the pattern for pairing celestial and terrestrial globes. This globe appears to be the model used by Holbein in his painting 'The Ambassadors'.
Science Museum, London

GERARD MERCATOR'S CELESTIAL GLOBE
1551. This globe shows a noticeable advance
on that of Schöner. It is centred on the equatorial poles rather than the ecliptic poles,
making it more closely analogous to the motion
of the celestial sphere, although the constellations are still portrayed in classical mirror-
image form. Still based on Ptolemy's astronomy, nearly all the one thousand stars in his
catalogue are marked. A product of the foremost terrestrial cartographer of his day, the
draughtsmanship is of a high standard, and the
constellation figures are clothed in classical
Roman dress. This was a highly influential
globe which sold in considerable numbers
throughout northern Europe down to the
1590s.

The National Maritime Museum, London

during centuries of medieval western neglect, and this tradition is then received by a
north European artist and given an elegant graphic form which satisfies the quickened
visual imagination of the Renaissance. The Dürer figures were copied by Peter Apian but
cleverly combined into a single sphere for the star map in his monumental work
Astronomicon Caesareum, 1540. This famous work was one of the most sumptuous
productions of the first century of printing. Apian created a series of revolving paper
models called volvelles, in which the movement of discs pinned at their centres
simulated those of the celestial bodies. They were paper equivalents of the late medieval
instruments, for instance simple equatoria or the much more intricate albion of Richard
of Wallingford, which all aimed at finding planetary positions; the fact of their being
printed on paper has often led to their being described as maps. Apian's work was more

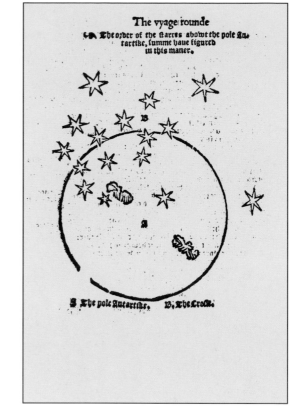

SOUTH POLAR STARS from Richard Eden's *Decades of the New World*, 1555. The Southern Cross and the Magellanic Clouds, drawn from an account of Magellan's voyage to latitude 55 degrees south during his circumnavigation of 1519–1522.
The British Library, C.13.a.8

astrological than astronomical in purpose, and the book definitely inhabits the pre-Copernican world. The volvelles were used for casting horoscopes and they made ingenious toys for Apian's wealthy patrons.

NEW INFLUENCES ON CELESTIAL MAPPING

Another class of astronomical image which was emphatically not new but which was now transformed by the medium of printing was the portrayal of the constellations. The first printed book of star maps was Alessandro Piccolomini's *De la Stelle Fisse* of 1540, but the use here of the term map is debatable: Piccolomini's stark star-groups, with no constellation-figures, have an austere, scientific appearance; but without printed co-ordinates (although they were clearly planned with co-ordinates to hand) they can no more be located on the celestial sphere than Al-Sufi's could be four centuries earlier. A definite advance appears in Giovanni Gallucci's *Theatrum Mundi* of 1588 where the constellations are drawn within a framework of co-ordinates and a geometric projection.

THE CAPRAROLA FRESCO, 1575, painted by an anonymous artist in the Villa Farnese at Caprarola. A secular form of the medieval frescos of heaven, this is a unique large-scale portrayal of the classical constellations in the context of private decorative art. But it is also of scientific interest as a projection: the artist must have had before him a celestial globe as he planned the layout of the painting, which measures approximately twelve metres by six.

The northern and southern heavens have been ingeniously combined on one plane by projecting the sphere as if it were the surface of a cylinder. The ecliptic is the wavy band across the width of the painting, and the polar regions are stretched out horizontally. The constellations are classically modelled, and the artist has added the figures of Jupiter and of Phaeton falling from his chariot.
Photograph: Scala

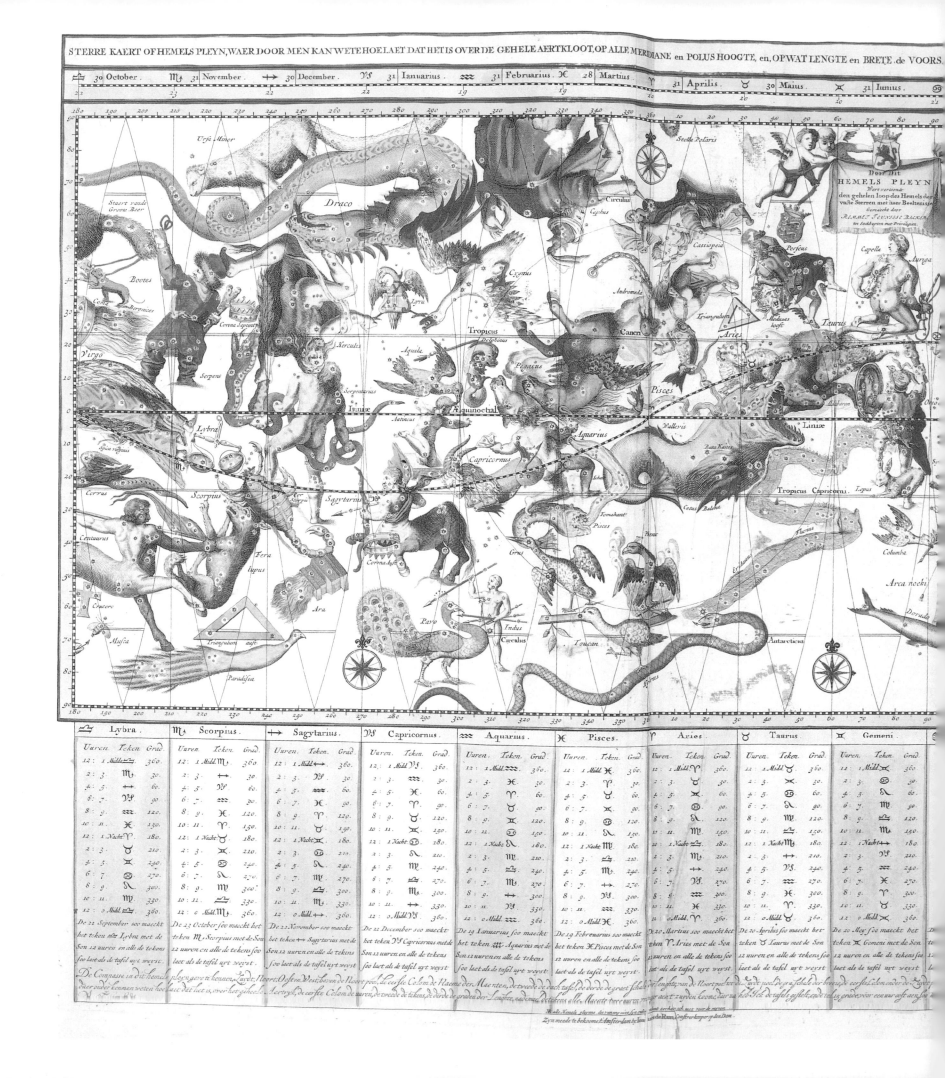

Building on the foundations laid by Dürer and Gallucci, the printed star charts of the next three centuries bear eloquent witness to the evolution of both the astronomy and the publishing taste of their day. New constellations were added, the moon was mapped, and the Copernican planetary system gained universal acceptance. Ptolemy's star catalogue was at last superseded and a series of landmark celestial atlases set ever new standards of fullness, accuracy and gracefulness. Geographical exploration, politics, religion, and the artistic styles of the time all left their mark on the evolving star map. Comets, eclipses, solar transits and nebulae were recorded and publicized as the star chart entered the mainstream of scientific life and of popular publishing. Like terrestrial maps and like other forms of technical publication (architecture for example, or medicine), star charts developed in a dual context. On the one hand leading astronomers such as Hevelius, Flamsteed and Bode were advancing the science of astronomy through innovative charts based on original research, while on the other hand resourceful publishers like Cellarius and Ottens were marketing well-designed but derivative star maps for a wider, educated audience. Elegant, compact and intellectually satisfying, maps of the northern and southern heavens became almost as familiar as the map of the world, and essential features in any library.

Contemporary with the appearance of the first printed star charts were the earliest globes, both celestial and terrestrial. Knowledge of the sphericity of the earth was widespread in the middle ages (contrary to modern popular belief), but the impulse to make three-dimensional models of the world from the late fifteenth century onwards stemmed directly from the great period of discovery and the sense of the world encompassed. The classical concept of the celestial sphere as enclosing the terrestrial was revived, and complementary models of the earth and the heavens were produced. Islamic scholars and craftsmen had never made terrestrial globes, but had for centuries made celestial ones, which by the sixteenth century were well known and admired in Europe. These had been skilfully made by the technically difficult process of metal casting. When German craftsmen devised the simpler method of moulding papier-maché around a carved ball, the moment was ripe for the production of globe pairs, matching the earth to its cosmic setting among the stars. The globe would always be more costly to make than a map, and for that reason it acquired a symbolic value as an emblem of scholarship married with wealth, and as such we encounter it in pictures such as Holbein's 'Ambassadors' of 1533. The novelty of the celestial globe even in Renaissance Italy may be gauged from Raphael's great fresco 'The School of Athens' c.1510, where an unidentified philosopher can plainly be seen holding a celestial globe, but where the artist has made no attempt to paint the actual stars or constellations realistically; unlike Holbein two decades later, he had no model to work from or felt that the figure of the pictorial globe would still be unfamiliar. The ultimate use of maps of the heavens (and of the earth) as displays of power may be seen in the vogue for mural decorations such as those in the Villa Farnese at Caprarola, where the possession of a private image of heaven seems to symbolize not merely the Farnese family's grasp on the things of this

BACKER'S STAR CHART, c.1710. An ingenious application of the Mercator-type projection to the celestial map. The heavenly sphere is conceived to be peeled back from the poles to form a cylinder, with the poles becoming complete circular bands. The cylinder is then unrolled to yield a rectangular map 180 degrees × 360 degrees, exactly analogous to the Mercator world map. The centre of the projection is the vernal equinox point, where the celestial equator crosses the ecliptic (again analogous to the centre of the world map where the Greenwich meridian crosses the equator). As a reference model displaying the relative positions of the stars and constellations, it is eminently useful; but like the Mercator world map, it is remote from the shape of the sphere, and from anything the human eye can see.
The Library of Congress, Washington D.C.

GLOBI COELESTIS IN TABULAS PLANAS REDACTI

in qua Longitudines Stellarum fixarum ad anum Christi completum 1730 tam Arithmetice quam Geometric
á IOH. GABR. DOPPELMAYR MATH. P.P. Academ. Cæs. Leopold: Car. Nat. Curiosorum, nec non Societatis Regiæ Borussicæ
Operâ IOH. BAPT. HOMANNI SAC. CÆS. MAJ. GEOGR. Norimbergæ.

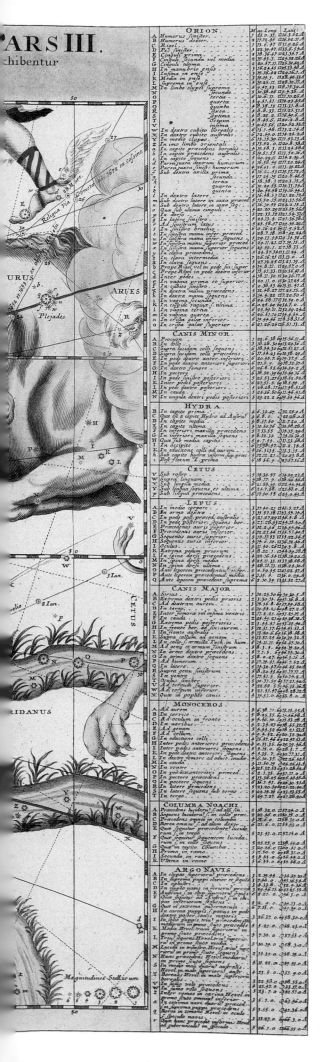

OTTENS'S REGIONAL SKY CHART, 1729. Prepared by a distinguished mathematician, Johann Doppelmayr, this is one of six detailed sky charts in which regions of the sky are ingeniously projected into rectangular maps. The projection used is the gnomonic, which has the interesting property that any straight line on the map is part of a great circle. This makes Doppelmayr's charts highly practical as observational aids, since a directional line on the map will correspond to an imaginary line from star to star in the sky, clearly not the case with a planisphere of the entire heavens. Doppelmayr provides a full star catalogue, correct for the epoch 1730.

The Library of Congress, Washington D.C.

HOLBEIN'S *AMBASSADORS*, 1533. Celestial and terrestrial globes as symbols of power and learning. The celestial globe closely resembles the Schöner globe. (Detail.)

The National Gallery, London

world, but their equality with the mythical heroes of the skies.

At the other extreme from the large globe as intellectual library furniture were the miniature models designed for the gentleman's, and perhaps for the mariner's, pocket. A terrestrial globe just two or three inches in diameter nestled inside a spherical case, on whose inner concave surface were drawn the northern and southern heavens. Largely a novelty testifying to the eighteenth-century vogue for the science of astronomy, they might still have been some practical use for demonstration purposes on sea or land. From ancient times the stars had of course been fundamental to marine navigation, the Plough (Ursa Major) and the pole star forming permanent markers for all Mediterranean seafarers. Although supplemented in the fifteenth century by compass and chart, seaborne expansion beyond European waters gave even greater importance to stellar navigation. The relationship between the celestial pole and the observer's horizon in fixing one's position was easily understood: the elevation of the pole at any point of observation is equal to that point's angular distance from the equator — its latitude. This theory had been expressed three centuries before in Sacrobosco's *De Sphaere*. Yet in order to put into effect this fundamental rule, an established latitude system was clearly essential, both celestial and terrestrial. Celestial navigation in this precise sense does not therefore predate the late fifteenth century when co-ordinate systems became familiar and began to appear on sea-charts, and when instruments for determining altitudes began to proliferate — the quadrant, the cross-staff, and the mariner's astrolabe. The last was much simpler than the astronomer's astrolabe, and was used to measure the altitude of the sun as it crossed the noon meridian, a technique increasingly employed as mariners voyaged out of sight of the pole star. It is sometimes thought that the age of discovery

BLAEU-GOLIUS GLOBE GORES, 1600 (1630). The surface map of printed celestial (and terrestrial) globes was drawn up in the form of 'gores' — the series of almond-shaped sections which can be joined to cover a globe-ball. This globe by Blaeu was one of the first to show the newly-chartered southern constellations described by Keyser. The grand, baroque style of Blaeu's constellation figures was to be seminal for all future makers of star charts.
Bodleian Library, Oxford, Vet. B3 b.29(2)

and consequent demands on navigation stimulated astronomers to devise new instruments, new observational skills and new theories, but there appears to be little direct correlation between the two. Navigational advances proceeded very much from pragmatic necessity, until the late seventeenth century at least, and sprang from within the maritime community. The revolution in empirical astronomy associated with Tycho, Kepler and Galileo was purely intellectual and scientific, having no connection with maritime enterprise, although of course their work would later have profound repercussions for navigation and geography generally. It was to be many years, the late seventeenth century at the earliest, before a new professionalism in maritime training would require the seafarer to have a thorough grasp of astronomy before he could be called a navigator.

Changes in instrumentation during the seventeenth century led to a shift from the use of the ecliptic co-ordinate system to the equatorial system, so that stellar latitude

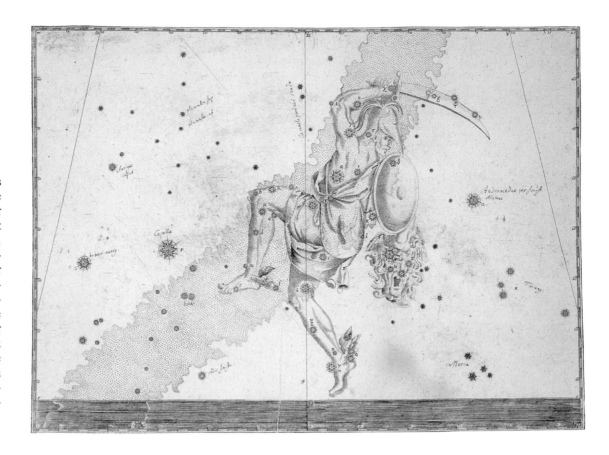

BAYER'S *URANOMETRIA*, 1603. Bayer's was the first engraved star atlas, and his maps have noticeably more precision than the earlier woodcuts of Gallucci. Bayer used the best contemporary star catalogue, that of Tycho, and he included the newly-designated southern constellations of Pieter Keyser. Bayer made the rational decision to portray the constellations as seen from earth. Another innovation introduced by Bayer was to classify the stars within each group according to their magnitude by using the letters of the greek alphabet, so that for example Mirfak, the bright star in Perseus's side, becomes alpha Perseus. This concept soon became indispensable to astronomers as a stellar reference system.

The British Library, Maps C.10.a.17, f.11

and longitude were directly analogous to those on earth. There is no great intellectual significance in the change: it was simply found more convenient, nor did the change occur suddenly, for throughout the period 1550–1750 either system might be used, so that one has to look carefully at any given chart or globe to determine whether it is projected from a celestial ecliptic or equatorial pole. It means that a star map entitled 'Northern Celestial Hemisphere' may not show the northern skies in our sense because the ecliptic will form the map's edge and extend to a point 23 degrees south of the equator. It was not until the late eighteenth century that the equatorial system became virtually universal. In both systems celestial longitude was measured from the vernal equinox point, latitude with reference to the relevant baseline — either the equatorial or the ecliptic.

The other technical matter which the makers of star charts had to consider was projection. In the case of world map projections, the sixteenth century saw intense and varied experimentation as cartographers sought to portray on paper their radically expanding world. One of the controlling factors was the natural desire to place Europe at the centre of the map and then to reach out from the old world to show the new discoveries to the east and the west. But the mapmaker always felt it essential to show the entire world, so that his problem became complex and capable of a great variety of solutions. In the case of the star chart there was far less experimentation, mainly because celestial chartmakers attempted to portray only one half of the sky. The central feature was always conceived to be the north or south celestial pole around which the heavens resolved. It was natural to choose the pole as the centre of the projection and to chart the stars as if the observer were looking down on the celestial sphere from a point high above the pole. The process of drawing the chart may then be visualized as if viewing a dome on which the stars appear, and which must then be spread out and transferred to a flat surface. It will be easily seen that as one progresses away from the central point of tangency, problems of compression and distortion will increase, and a decision must be taken how far from the pole to continue the chart. The solution is to stretch the map progressively away from the pole so that an entire hemisphere down to the equator or even the tropic of Capricorn may be shown. The problems of projecting the celestial sphere on to paper are identical to those of projecting the spherical earth, but at an early stage the polar projection established itself as the norm for star charts and there were few departures from this rule (perhaps the most interesting is the map designed in 1684 by Remmet Backer, which is an ingenious equivalent of the Mercator projection world map). Maps of the entire northern or southern heavens were not observational instruments; they were convenient conceptual models, or reference charts, and were accepted as such by their scientific users. But in general celestial mapmakers felt that no purpose would have been served by experimenting with a variety of new celestial projections, since the pragmatic fact that the starry sphere was never seen in its entirety was accepted as according with our senses and our reason. The polar projection as it appears in the first star charts could be considered as an interesting early use of perspective, but instead of being used to foreshorten and compress, optical geometry is used to expand the two-dimensional space available to the artist. The maps of individual constellations which filled celestial atlases were effectively regional star charts, analogous to maps of individual countries in an atlas of the world, in which the problems of projection were correspondingly less severe.

Celestial charts were undoubtedly more conservative documents than most other forms of map, so that the broad structure of the first manuscript planisphere of 1440 is still dominant in an eighteenth-century star chart. But within this framework of strong continuity, there was a process of variation, elaboration, and refinement, as well as short-lived experiments and a few permanent transformations. Since the appearance of Ptolemy's star catalogue around the year 150AD no astronomers for 1,400 years had ventured to add to his 48 constellations. Challenges to this status quo obviously arose first with the voyages of discovery and second with the movement to recatalogue the stars which began with Tycho. From around 1450 Portuguese mariners in search of a sea-route to the east voyaged steadily further south along the coast of Africa until Dias rounded the Cape in 1489. Obviously these sailors lost sight of almost all their familiar stars, and they must have quickly identified others to sail by. Yet from all the Portuguese and Spanish seafaring enterprise of the sixteenth century, almost no records of star sightings or new constellations have survived. Vespucci's narratives of his Atlantic voyages, published from 1504 onwards, contained small figures of a handful of new stars, while the remnants of Magellan's crew told of two detached clouds of light visible far to the south and apparently detached from the Milky Way. The Portuguese navigator Cadomosto reported near the mouth of the river Gambia, at 13 degrees north, that the Pole star sank so low that it touched the sea, while to the south an outstanding group of stars in the form of a cross appeared — the first reference to the Southern Cross. These are all the direct astronomical results of these pioneering voyages. We must assume that the Portuguese who were sailing the Cape route and the Indian Ocean throughout the sixteenth century did in fact identify new guiding-stars, but that some motive — perhaps a desire for secrecy — prevented their publication. It was not until 1595–96 during Frederik de Houtman's voyage via the Cape to Java, that his Dutch compatriot, the navigator Pieter Dircksz Keyser, systematically formed a host of southern stars into twelve new constellations. He chose to name most of them after exotic beasts, some mythical like the Chameleon and the Phoenix, others native to the newly explored territories of South Asia, the Toucan, the Bird of Paradise and the Flying Fish. On Keyser's return to Europe these were published in textual form with the star co-

NAVIGATION, from Pedro da Medina's *Regimiento de Navigacion*, 1563. A mariner uses a cross-staff to determine the altitude of the Pole Star above the horizon, and hence his latitude.

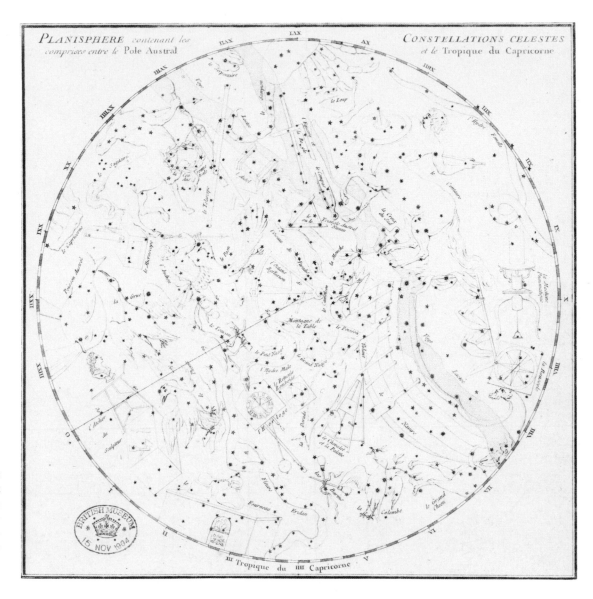

LACAILLE'S CONSTELLATIONS, 1752. The French astronomer Nicolas de Lacaille spent the years 1750–52 surveying the southern skies from the Cape Observatory. He designated thirteen new constellations based on scientific instruments. His were the last new constellations to win universal acceptance.
The British Library, Maps 141.a.1.(20)

ordinates, and in graphic form on celestial globes made by Hondius and Blaeu in the last years of the century. They became more generally known through Johann Bayer's great star atlas *Uranometria* of 1603, and they have become permanent.

This mood of innovation seems to have communicated itself to other astronomers, for in 1624 Jakob Bartsch (Kepler's son-in-law) formed a number of previously detached stars into new northern constellations, the Giraffe, the Dove and the Unicorn. In 1687 Johannes Hevelius of Gdansk designated a further seven groups, almost all northern, including the Lynx, the Fox and the Hunting Dogs. The last permanent block of constellations to be designated by an individual astronomer was the creation of Nicolas de Lacaille who spent the years 1751–2 surveying the southern sky from the Cape of Good Hope. Working consciously in the spirit of eighteenth-century science, Lacaille turned his back on traditional animal motifs and chose instead technical subjects, the Clock, the Compass, the Telescope and so on.

Although Lacaille was the last individual to leave the products of his imagination permanently in the map of the skies, there were many other attempts to create new constellation which failed to win recognition from the world of astronomy, and these attempts reflect the intellectual and sometimes the social context in which astronomers

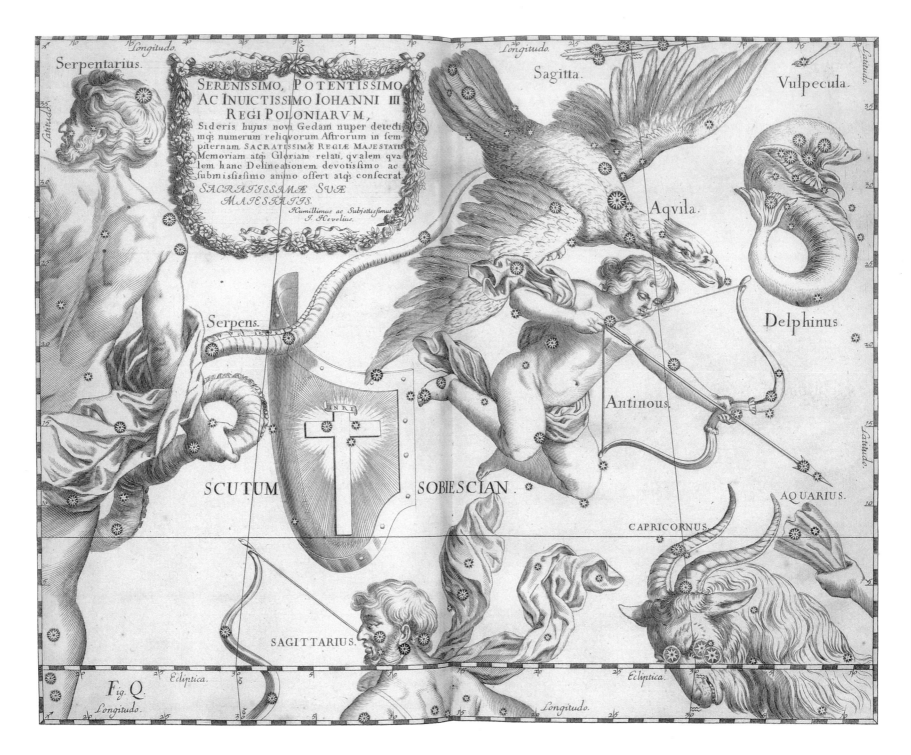

Serpentarius.

SERENISSIMO, POTENTISSIMO AC INUICTISSIMO IOHANNI III REGI POLONIARVM, Sideris hujus novi Gedani nuper detecti, mq̃ numerum reliqvorum Astrorum in sempiternam SACRATISSIMÆ REGIÆ MAJESTATIS Memoriam atq̃ Gloriam relati, qvalem qvalem hanc Delineationem devotissimo ac submississimo animo offert atq̃ consecrat. *SACRATISSIMÆ SVÆ MAJESTATIS.* Humillimus ac Subjectissimus J. Hevelius.

Sagitta.

Vulpecula.

Aqvila.

Serpens.

Delphinus.

SCUTUM

SOBIESCIAN

Antinous.

AQUARIUS.

CAPRICORNUS.

SAGITTARIUS.

Fig. Q.

HEVELIUS the sword and shield of Jan Sobieski, King of Poland.

were working. One prominent theme or motive in the design of new constellations was the quest for political favour or patronage, understandable perhaps in an age when kings and nobles were the only possible source for the endowment and support of observatories. The French astronomers Pardies and Royer proposed a Fleur de Lys and a Sceptre to honour Louis XIV. Godfried Kirch invented Swords, Sceptres and Orbs in honour of various German royal houses. In Restoration England, Edward Sherburne and Edmond Halley devised respectively a Royal Heart and a Royal Oak in commemoration of Charles I and Charles II. Given their strongly partisan character, none of these symbols was likely to win permanent acceptance among the international scientific community.

Perhaps the most ambitious of all the products of this political astronomy was the plan of Erhard Weigel in Jena in the 1680s to replace all the classical constellations with the coats of arms of the ruling houses of Europe.

It is easy to forget that there was a serious motive behind the creation of new constellations: the desire for completeness and the desire for new and more accurate star catalogues. The classic catalogues of Ptolemy and Tycho made reference only to some 1,000 stars grouped into the familiar 48 constellations; but what of the thousands of other stars which lay between constellations, the so-called unformed stars, how were they to be catalogued with no star-group or sky-region to locate them? There were substantial empty spaces, even in the northern sky, so that for example Hevelius's motive in creating the constellation Canes Venatici — the Hunting Dogs — was to impose some plan on

WEIGEL'S POLITICAL CONSTELLATIONS, 1688. Many new constellations were devised by astronomers to honour royal patrons, but none of these innovations was as radical as Erhard Weigel's scheme for replacing the entire face of the classical heavens with the coats of arms of Europe's royal houses — the German eagle, the French fleur de lys, and so on. Weigel was a professor at the university of Jena, and a distinguished mathematician, and we must assume that his published proposal was in earnest. However, like most politically-inspired constellations, it failed to win acceptance.

The British Library, Maps K.6.5, plate 111

the area of sky between Ursa Major and Boötes. This may be thought of as analogous to the increasingly large scale of terrestrial maps, so that more detail could be represented.

No less radical than the political constellations, but also doomed to failure, was the scheme to de-paganize the heavens, to replace the mythological and animal figure with Christian and Biblical subjects. This project took two forms; on the simpler level the 1655 celestial maps of Wilhelm Schickard reproduced the familiar figures, but added brief texts suggesting ingenious Biblical equivalents for them. Cepheus for example is compared to Solomon, Perseus to David, Draco to the dragon in Revelation. This idea

SCHILLER: CYGNUS AS THE HOLY CROSS, 1627. Perhaps the most intriguing attempt to replace the traditional constellations was that of the German scholar Julius Schiller. Allotting the northern heavens to the New Testament and the southern to the Old Testament, Schiller found biblical and ecclesiastical replacements for all the classical star-groups. Their failure to win acceptance even in Catholic countries demonstrates the tenacity of classical traditions in European art and science.
The British Library, 562*e.23, p.47

was fully worked out and given dramatic visual expression in the *Coelum Stellatum Christianum* of Julius Schiller published in 1627, who devised a radically Christianized map of the heavens. Schiller's southern hemisphere was transformed into a cavalcade of Old Testament subjects — Job takes the place of the Indian and the Peacock, the Centaur is transformed into Abraham and Isaac, and so on. The northern heavens are filled with New Testament and Christian imagery: Cassiopeia becomes Mary Magdalen, Perseus St Paul, while the twelve Zodiac signs are conveniently replaced by the twelve apostles. Schiller's maps reached a high standard of detail and precision; they were certainly not intended to be capricious or ephemeral, yet his innovations failed to persuade his contemporaries, perhaps the heavily Catholic nature of his imagery being at fault, and his work is now only an intriguing footnote in the history of astronomy. It

QVADRANS MVRALIS
SIVE TICHONICVS.

TYCHO BRAHE, 1598. A famous picture of the great astronomer in his observatory. Tycho's work was pretelescopic, and the large mural quadrant with which he observed all his star positions is seen in the foreground.
The British Library, C.54.h.3.

is difficult not to sympathize with Schiller, for surely the desire to Christianize the heavens was neither an eccentric nor a controversial ambition, and he might legitimately have expected to succeed in Christian Europe. Schiller's constellations were contemporary with the elaborate scenes of heaven painted on the ceilings of baroque churches in Catholic Europe, and his maps underline the paradox of the survival throughout the Christian centuries of the pagan, animistic sky-figures.

THE CLASSICAL AGE OF STAR MAPS

Of far greater permanent value than these experiments were the series of great celestial atlases, each of which in turn set new standards of fullness and accuracy. The woodcut atlases of Piccolomini and Gallucci were extremely important in their way, but a glance at Johann Bayer's atlas *Uranometria*, published in Augsburg in 1603, reveals immediately a different order of achievement. The medium of copper-plate engraving created a much more precise image than the woodcut, and, in the hands of the skilled engraver, the modelling of the constellation figures has a rich, sculptural quality. Bayer had access to the new star catalogue of Tycho, which could claim to be the first new star survey of the modern age. Although Bayer does not show a dramatically increased number of stars compared with Gallucci, each one is precisely located and graded for magnitude, and it was in this atlas that Bayer introduced for the first time the system of ordering the stars within each constellation by the letters of the Greek alphabet. This excellent principle was not universally imitated until the following century. Johannes Hevelius's atlas *Uranographia* of 1687 consolidated the approach of Bayer, and first showed the seven new constellations of his own devising. Even at this date Hevelius preferred non-telescopic instruments to sight the stars, and during a visit from Edmond Halley to his observatory in Gdansk, Hevelius attempted to demonstrate that he could take more accurate stellar positions than Halley could with a telescope. It was Hevelius too who had the distinction of publishing the first atlas of the moon, *Selenographia*, 1647. Constructed from his own observations, this time with a telescope, it displayed for the first time the complexity of moon's topography, although it perpetuated certain myths such as the existence of lunar seas. Few of the place-names proposed by Hevelius became permanent, indeed one of the most striking aspects of his maps is the elaborate analogy he built up between the topography of the moon and that of the earth, with the Mediterranean, North Africa and Asia Minor dominating the moon's visible face. It is to the Jesuit astronomer, Giambattista Riccioli, an ardent opponent of Copernicanism, that we owe most of the familiar lunar names.

The foundations for a new area of research vital for the development of astronomy were laid between 1770 and 1785 when Charles Messier began the observation and charting of nebulae. What began as an offshoot from Messier's interest in comet-hunting — a widespread addiction among eighteenth-century astronomers — culminated in the

SCHILLER: THE CHRISTIANIZED HEAVENS, 1660. Schiller himself did not publish general maps of his Christianized heavens, but some years later Andreas Cellarius did. Here, the southern hemisphere is filled with Old Testament figures such as Job, Aaron and the angel Raphael, while the north shows St Paul, Jerome, and others. The Zodiac figures along the ecliptic have been transformed into the twelve apostles. The map and its twin adopt an unusual structure: instead of being projected from the poles they centre on the equinoxes. The ecliptic bisects the map instead of encircling it, and each hemisphere shows part of the northern and the southern sky. These maps are exactly analogous to the twin-hemisphere world map that was prevalent during the seventeenth century.
The British Library, Maps C.6.c.2

93

identification of 109 star clusters, nebulae or galaxies, and the recognition of the importance of these bodies in understanding the heavens. Messier himself did not embody his researches into an atlas of nebulae but he had the rare distinction of identifying a whole new class of objects in the sky for future mapmakers to chart. Comet-hunting also gave rise to a positive torrent of publications showing the shape and position of the latest visitor from space. Some of these were ephemeral broadsheets, while the major atlas publishers vied with each other to design elaborate diagrams of comets passing the earth against the starry background.

New standards were set by John Flamsteed, the first Astronomer Royal in Britain, whose *Atlas Coelestis* of 1729 contained maps of the 25 constellations visible from Greenwich. Based on his own catalogue of nearly 4,000 stars, it was unprecedented in

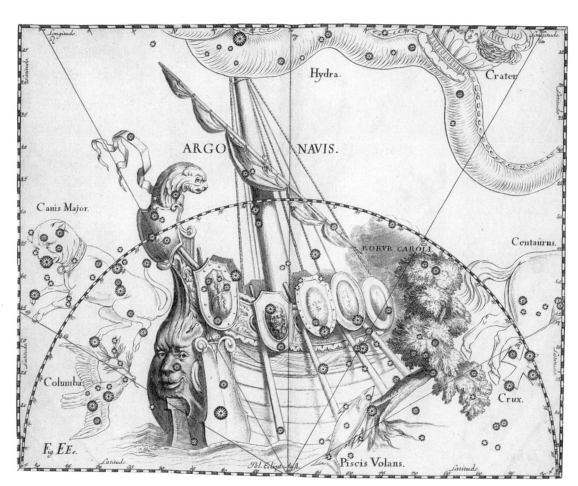

HEVELIUS: ARGO from *Uranographia*, 1690. Johannes Hevelius's star catalogue of more than 1,500 stars was the most comprehensive of its time, and it formed the basis of his great celestial atlas. He designated seven new and permanent constellations, including the sextant (the first scientific subject) and the shield of his Polish King, Jan Sobieski. He included others which had a short life-span, such as 'Charles' Oak', seen here, which he copies from his English colleagues. Unlike Bayer, Hevelius reverted to the classical reverse orientation of the constellations.
The British Library, 532.K.19

its detail, and the graceful, classically-modelled engravings were designed by one of the foremost artists of the day, Sir James Thornhill, who had created murals in many of Wren's great buildings including St Paul's Cathedral and the Greenwich Hospital. The starting-point for Flamsteed's lifelong observations has often been retold: that in the quest for a means of determining longitude — a vital but elusive prize among the maritime nations — astronomers had suggested that the heavens might be used as a natural clock. The theory was that, for example, regular changes in the size and position of the moon could be observed and tabulated at a standard meridian. Mariners at sea might then compare what they saw with these standard tables, and calculate the time

HEVELIUS'S PANTHEON from *Uranographia*, 1690. The conscious excitement of the new age of empirical astronomy is reflected in this gallery of modern astronomers, Copernicus and Tycho, on a par with the ancient authorities, Ptolemy and Hipparchus.

difference between the two, each hour's difference representing 15 degrees of longitude. The theory was perfectly sound, but when Flamsteed was asked for his opinion, he replied that the accuracy with which the movements of the moon had hitherto been measured was totally inadequate to the demands of this scheme. This was the background to the establishment of the Royal Observatory, within which Flamsteed set out to create a new body of astronomical data for the new age of science. The striking thing about Flamsteed's star catalogue and his atlas was that they were derived from the first telescopic sky survey, since those of Tycho and Hevelius had both been optical only, using naked-eye sightings with large quadrants. Flamsteed's instruments were

TABULA SELENOGRAPHIC[A]

in qua

Lunarium Macularum exacta Descriptio secundum Nomenclaturam
Præstantissimorum Astronomorum

tam

HEVELII quam RICCIOLI

Curiosis Rei Sidereæ Cultoribus exhibetur

à

Ioh. Gabr. Doppelmajero Math. P.P.

opera

Ioh. Baptistae Homanni

Norinbergæ.

Nullum inter corpora cælestia, ex quo tempore Veteres sacræ Uraniæ addicti omne moverant lapidem, ut Siderum naturæ & affectiones quam maxime forent, in aprico posita, cunctorum viret magis admirationem, & multiformi ambage (si cum Plinio loqui liceat) torsit contemplantium ingenia, proximum quippe ignorari sidus indignantiu, quam ipsa Luna, varietate macularum imprimis miranda; sed nec mirari nos subeat, cum medijs tunc destituti, quibus nunc Lunam accuratius inspicere & contemplari nobis hodie datum, oculis scilicet armatis; hinc etiam deficiente hoc Tuborum opticorum apparatu diversas de Lunæ substantia è maculis nudo oculo visis fovere opiniones non potuere non Antiqui illi rei sidereæ Cultores; alij enim cum Cleardo & Argesinaeo maculas Lunares nostri Oceani imaginem in Luna tanquam in speculo conspicuam esse, alii hasce è certis corporibus, quæ Solem inter & Lunam jaceant originem ducere existimarunt; alii Lunam vitream, non quidem exacte pellucidá, sed ex parte opacam; alii partim igneam, partim opacam putarunt; & quæ sunt multæ aliæ de corporis Lunaris substantia sententiæ.

At multo feliciori successu omnium primus celeberrimus ille Florentinorum Mathematicus Galilæus de Galileis anno superioris seculi decimo, quo utilissimu Tuborum opticorum inventum luci publicæ traditum, id negotium tentavit. quod dein Scheinerus & alii satis superq; dedere probatum, imo plures hodie Tubis prædictis ad majorem perfectionem nunc perductis, rem acu, quod ajunt, multo felicius tangere videntur, si proin dubio asserunt, quod Luna innumeris scateat montibus, qui nostros altitudine, habito respectu globi Lunaris ad nostrum, sexagies fere mino-

ris, superent; porro quod eædem profunditates, quæ prægrandibus semper in ambitu suo exteriori, plerumque circulari, mæniorum instar, cinguntur eminentijs, innumeras fere et multò plures sed non tantas et tam profundas, quam nostra exhibet Terra, si huius cavitates suis destituerentur maribus; denique quod partes multæ in Luna obscuræ, quæ sub primo conspectu non apparent profunde, ideoq; pro materia liquida, maribus scilicet multorum forsan judicio censendæ, adhibita accuratiori inspectione, teste Viro celeberrimo Dno de la Hire, nihilominus profunde nec tamen liquide deprehendantur; uthinc haud pauci cum acutissimo Galilæo Lunam pro corpore materiam à Terra diversam habente existimare possent, in qua etiam fortasse substantiæ & res creatæ existant, quæ operationes edant ab imaginatione nostra, sicut remotus, ita & prorsus alienas; quippe quæ nullam cum nostris similitudinem habeant, & proin omnino sint à nostra cogitatione discrepantes.

Quamvis autem Luna profunditatibus & eminentiis quamplurimis sit referta, sæpissime tamen contingit; superficiem Lunæ in certis à Sole distantiis adeò immutatam videri, ut magnus ille montium & profunditatum numerus, qui nuper admodum distinctissime observari potuerat, non amplius tunc sub conspectum cadat; ratio huius mutationis ex ipsa figura superiori A intermedia facile patescit, quod scilicet profunditates inter nonnullas et quadraturas, Luna crescente & dextris maxime, decrescente autem hac à sinistris potissimum altissimorum circumjacentium montium obtegantur umbris; et quidem quod insuper tales pro vario Solis ad Lunam positu perpetuo immutentur (quæ proinde etiam novæ maculæ denominari solent) emi-

nentiæ autem, cum Sol illas à latere illuminat, quam maxime conspicuæ dantur; cum è contrario à quadraturis ad oppositionem superficies Lunæ Sol hisce inæqualitatibus magis magisque verticaliter imminere pergit, et quidquid umbrosum ante fuit, pedetentim illuminat, aliam semper aciem, ut tandem luminosa et albicans appareat.

Ex hoc fundamento bina nostra Schemata in delineatione macularum notabilem etiam differentiam involvunt, eò quod primum, HEVELIANUM, in oppositione cum Sole existente, hoc est, in plenilunio designatum vero, RICCIOLINUM scilicet, è pluribus Lunæ phasibus in unum corpus collectum. In denominationibus macularum, utpote signis et significationibus contrarijs, dictos Auctores inter se differre hic in aperto videmus, cum Hevelius nomina marium, regionum, fluminum et montium nostrorum imitatus, Riccioli tem illustrium & de re siderea optime meritorum Astronomorum, comp præsertim sive Societatis Mathematicorum nomina pro usu Astronomi legerit.

Bini circa Lunam limbi se vicinem secantes nihil aliud, quam motus al Luna libratorii terminos, intra quos perpetua deprehenditur librationis subindicant; qui hodie demum per Tubos è diversa macularum nonnulla tutatione observatus, nec Veteribus olim notus fuit. eandem quippe nobis constantissime semper Lunam obvertere existimantibus; peragit autem tum suum libratorium per quatuordecim circiter dies trigesima sexta ti-

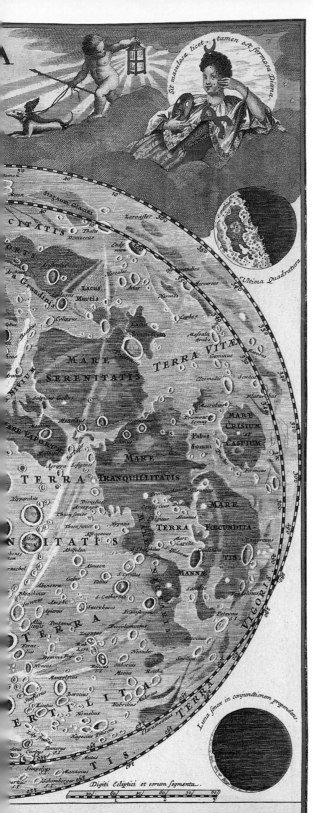

COR CAROLI from Philip Lea's chart of the northern heavens, 1686. The heart of the executed King Charles I, a constellation designed by the English royalist poet and scholar Edward Sherburne. Surely one of the most curious of all the politically-inspired constellations.

The British Library, Maps 20(84)

equipped with micrometers, and he achieved an accuracy of 10 seconds of arc, improving on Tycho's work by a factor of more than 10. The value of his observational work is clearly demonstrated by the eagerness with which the great theoretical scientists of his day, especially Newton, demanded access to it. Newton regarded the data which Flamsteed was accumulating as fundamental to his own continuing work on the problems of celestial mechanics, and in a bitter feud with Flamsteed, he virtually stole and published the data against Flamsteed's will. As with Tycho, it is interesting that the publication of celestial maps was not a priority with Flamsteed. He died in 1719 having completed virtually all the necessary observations for a new star catalogue, which appeared in three volumes in 1725. Finally his widow and one of his assistants published the atlas in 1729, as a memorial to the great observer and as an embodiment of his work which the non-specialist could appreciate.

The level of completeness sought by Flamsteed was extended to the rest of the heavens in the maps of Johann Bode. In his *Vorstellung der Gestirne* of 1782, Bode had built on Flamsteed's work, but extended to cover the southern skies, and produced an atlas of around 5,000 stars. But it was Bode's later *Uranographia* of 1801 which represents the high-point of pictorial star atlases, showing more than 15,000 stars in a series of clear and vigorous engravings, which took star maps for the first time to the limit of naked-eye visibility and beyond. Even with the multitude of recently-designated constellations, Bode's atlas is remarkable for the huge number of stars which lay between the figures, a fact which led to his inovative idea of constellation boundaries. Within a few decades

HOMANN'S MOON MAP, *c.*1730. It was Hevelius who, in his *Selenographia* of 1647, published the first atlas devoted to lunar maps. These had recorded his own telescopic observations from his observatory in Gdansk. Although he represented many topographical features accurately, his interpretation of what he saw created many fables, such as the existence of large seas on the moon. He conceived a fanciful correspondence between the geography of the moon and that of the earth, and named many lunar features after those on the earth. The currently accepted lunar names were devised later by the Jesuit scholar Riccioli. The ideal solution for map publishers was to print this dual image, setting Hevelius's map beside Riccioli's. The great southern crater makes them instantly distinguishable: it was Riccioli who named it Tycho, while Hevelius had likened it to Mount Sinai.

The Library of Congress, Washington D.C.

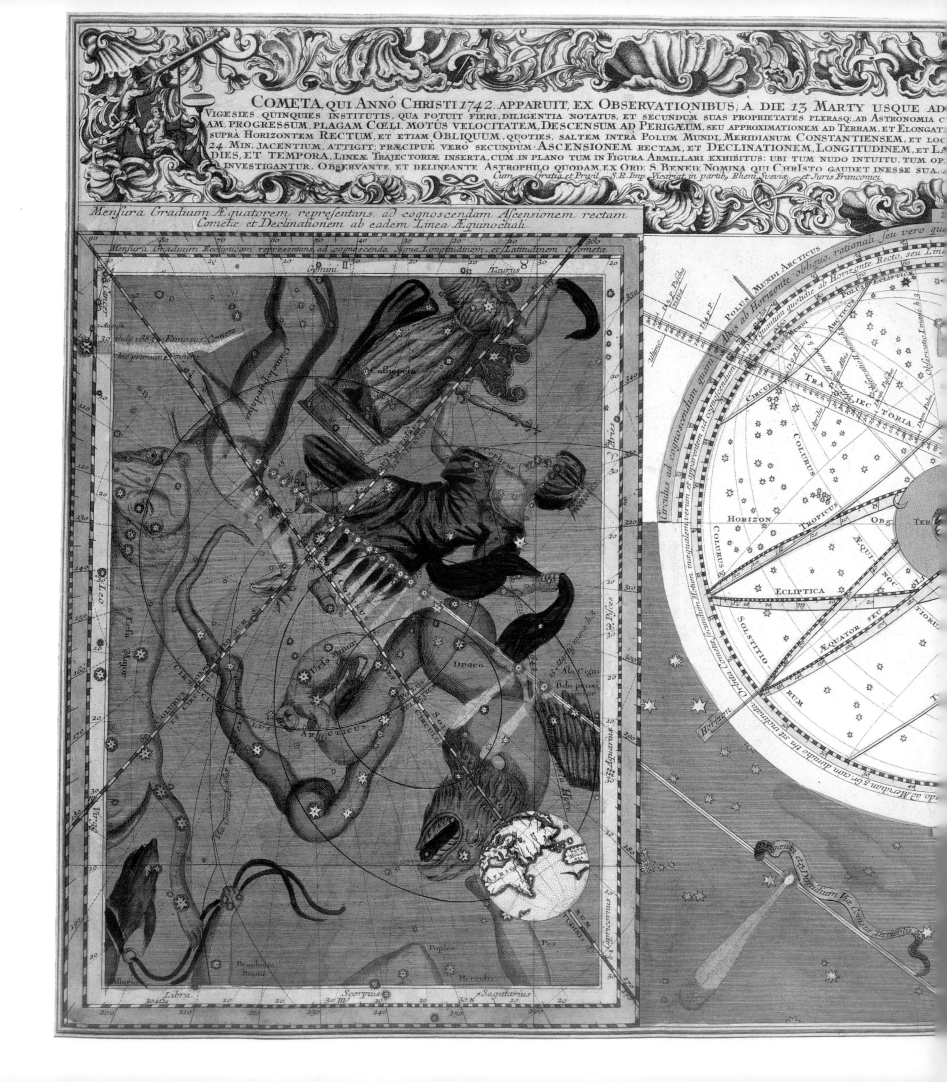

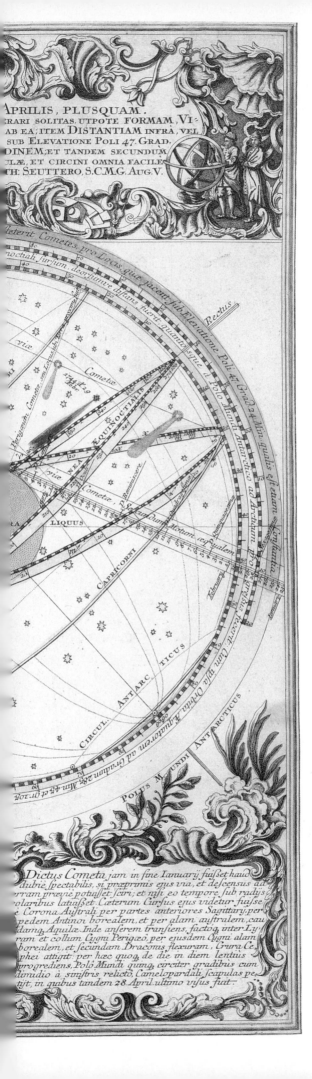

DAYLIGHT CLOCK, *c*.1740. An ingenious diagram revealing the reality behind the clock face: the earth is seen from above the pole, with the sunlight on half of the earth and the rest in darkness.
The British Library, Maps C.26.f.5

of the appearance of Bode's atlas, which had many imitators, astronomers began to feel that the pictorial representation of the constellations was a distracting anachronism, and during the nineteenth century a new, austere and functional form of star map appeared which dispensed with them. Pictorial star maps did not vanish, but they became confined to popular scientific publications, and professional astronomers no longer used them. Agreed constellation boundaries were plotted which divided the sky into recognized regions, and international astronomical societies co-operated to call a halt to the arbitrary invention of new constellations. Thus the process of artistic elaboration of the sky map, which had begun in the printed medium three centuries earlier with Dürer, was ended in the scientific realm, though not in the popular mind.

The artistic form of the published constellation figures naturally varies with the style and taste of their time: they might be noticeably Islamic or Christian, Medieval or Renaissance, Classical or Baroque. Provided that the stars themselves were shown in their correct mutual relationships, the actual style of the figures was naturally in the hands of the artist. One might expect an enormous variety of style and detail in the constellation images, yet through many centuries of pictorial star charts there remains a strong element of continuity, as though the artists were always aware that they were working within a long-established tradition. There was one stylistic problem which greatly exercised the makers of star charts over the years, namely whether the constellations should be pictured from the front or the rear. In his instructions on making a celestial globe, Ptolemy had argued logically that since we must see the model globe

SEUTTER: THE COMET OF 1742. For eighteenth-century scientists, comet-hunting was a favourite sport. Although comets were mysterious and apparently random in their appearance, Halley had demonstrated that they were indeed part of the solar system. Any new comet was eagerly studied for the light it might shed on planetary mechanics. Map publishers capitalized on this interest by issuing numerous charts of the paths of comets. This map by Mattheus Seutter of the comet that was visible from 13 March to 15 April 1742, is unusually imaginative in design, showing the path across the entire celestial sphere, and also in more detail its position during its 33 days of visibility in the constellations Draco and Cepheus.
The Library of Congress, Washington D.C.

PERSEUS

CASSIOPEIA

Algol

TRIANGULUM

TAURUS

ANDROMEDA

ARIES

FLAMSTEED'S *ATLAS COELESTIS*, 1729. Flamsteed was the moving spirit behind the foundation of the Royal Observatory at Greenwich. Ten years after his death this atlas was published from his catalogue of 3,000 stars visible from Greenwich. It was by far the fullest star catalogue published to that date, throughout the eighteenth century. The elegant engravings were executed by James Thornhill, and Flamsteed followed Bayer's Greek-letter system to catalogue the bright stars.

The British Library, Maps C.10.c.10, plate 16

from the outside and the earth is conceived to lie at its centre, the constellations must appear as they would from beyond the starry sphere, that is from the rear. But should this apply also to a map, about which Ptolemy gave no instructions? If followed, it produces the obvious problem that the star groups do not appear as seen from the earth, but as mirror-images, in which left and right are reversed. It also has the second important effect that it appears to throw the motion of the Zodiac into an anti-clockwise direction, instead of the clockwise progress observed from the earth. The medieval illustrations to Aratus or Hyginus were completely outside the Ptolemaic tradition, and they worked in the most natural way, showing the figures from the front. Curiously the Islamic globe-makers and astronomical illustrators such as Al-Sufi, who were steeped in the Ptolemaic works, nevertheless chose to ignore him on this point and depict the constellations from the front. When the first star charts were drawn in the fifteenth century, in the context of the revival of classical science, their authors interpreted Ptolemy's principle as indeed applying to star maps, and this justified the rear-view which Dürer adopted in his seminal work. During the next 300 years, this was the model which prevailed, although some mapmakers, Flamsteed for example, took the more pragmatic view that the constellations should be depicted as seen from the earth, that the classical rear-view was pedantic and lacking in sense. It is noticeable that both the newly-designated and the experimental constellations, those of Keyser and Schiller, took the opportunity to break with the classical convention.

The existence of this problem and the prevalence of the classical norm, illustrate the conservatism that marks the long history of the star chart. Just as medieval artists,

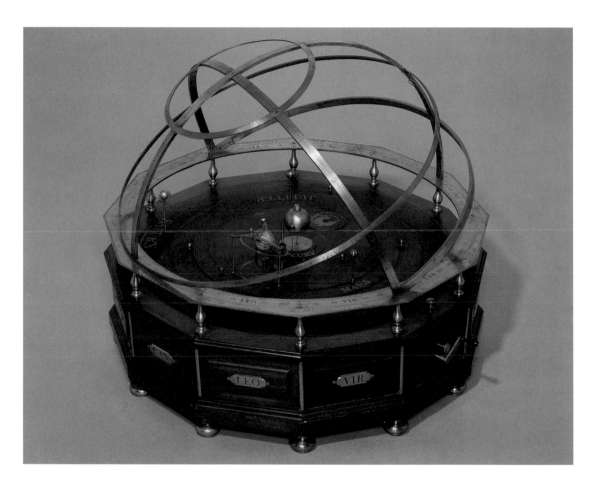

ORRERY. The first of these mechanical models of the solar system was probably invented under the patronage of Charles Boyle, 4th Earl of Orrery. From a viewpoint outside the solar system they presented the periods of planetary revolution accurately, but the scale of the orbits was necessarily compressed. Some models also showed the planetary moons. Similar models of the Sun-Earth-Moon system were produced, called Tellurians. They seem to embody the eighteenth-century perception of the cosmos as a rationally-designed mechanism.

Science Museum, London

Islamic or Christian, had taken a non-scientific delight in the constellation figures, so even in the scientific climate of the seventeenth and eighteenth centuries there were publishers who were motivated more by the aesthetics of the market-place than by a desire to serve science. The most elaborate and famous celestial atlas of the seventeenth century was issued by an author unknown to the history of astronomy. Andreas Cellarius's *Atlas Coelestis* (Amsterdam 1660) contained dozens of imaginatively designed plates showing the classical and Christianized heavens, the Ptolemaic and Copernican planetary systems, and experimental projections designed to simulate a three-dimensional view of the earth and the heavens. Cellarius's concept of a richly-illustrated collection of maps combined with astronomical diagrams, and aimed at the wider market outside the scientific professions, was imitated by several eighteenth-century map publishers, notably Homann in Nürnberg and Ottens in Amsterdam. But undoubtedly

CELLARIUS: SOUTHERN SKY, 1660. The *Atlas Coelestis* of Andreas Cellarius was an eclectic group of astronomical charts and diagrams, displaying many different and often contradictory views of the heavens. It was partly a historical reference work, explaining the planetary theories of Ptolemy, Copernicus and Tycho. Its elaborately designed celestial maps were essentially artistic variations on a theme. This plate offers a novel view of the earth, the Pacific and Antarctic regions, as if seen through the starry sphere, from a point in deep space. Undeniably ingenious, its practical use for astronomers is highly doubtful.

The British Library, Maps C.6.c.3

the most visually powerful and frankly artistic star charts ever made were those of the Venetian globe-maker Vincenzo Coronelli (1650–1718). Published in the form of gores (that is, oval sections which were cut and pasted to a globe) of various sizes, Coronelli's constellation figures are triumphs of late Baroque art: the sculptured forms seem replete with gigantic strength, and the darkly etched engravings create a series of dramatic tableaux totally removed from the little woodcut figures of Dürer or Honter. The publications of Cellarius, Homann and Ottens were hand-coloured after printing, and relied on the rich artistry of the colourist for much of their impact; by contrast, the strength of the Coronelli engravings is most impressive in their pristine state, although they were no doubt coloured when assembled into globes.

The iconographic style of the constellation figures within star charts does not present a line of clear chronological development, but a number of alternative traditions are discernible. Dürer's highly influential figures are, as one might expect, classically modelled in the main; for example his Perseus is naked like a Greek statue. On the other hand his Orion is armoured like a Teutonic knight of the sixteenth century, while

OTTENS: SOUTHERN SKY, 1729. Another chart designed by the German mathematician Johann Doppelmayr, this shows clearly the southern group of exotic constellations, the Indian, the Peacock the Toucan, etc., and some that did not become permanent, such as the Royal Oak and the Fly. The views of the European observatories, including Greenwich, indicate that the map was aimed at pleasing an educated lay public, rather than for use by professional astronomers.

The Library of Congress, Washington D.C.

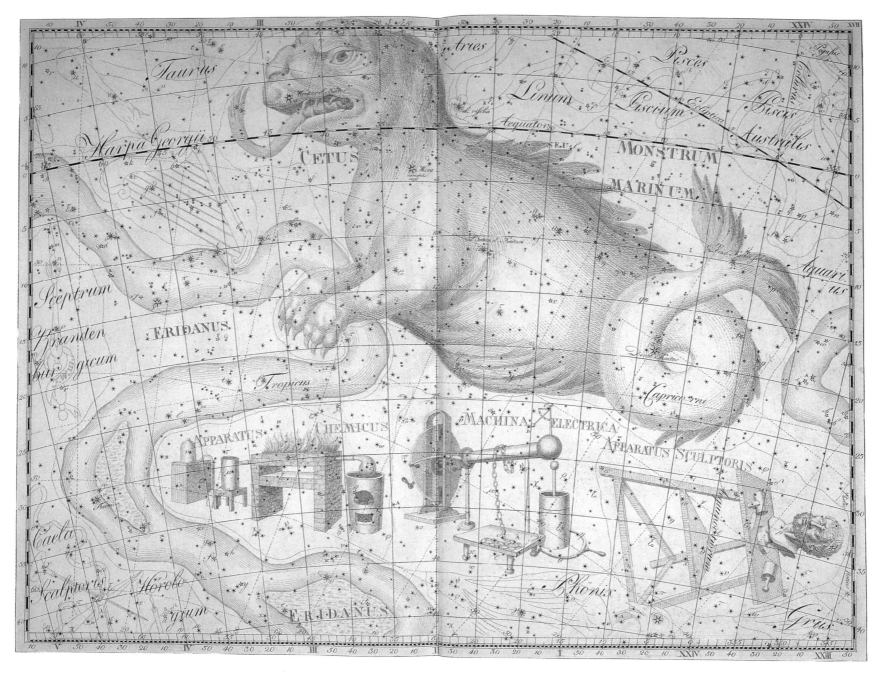

BODE: *URANOGRAPHIA*, 1801. Until the later nineteenth century Bode's remained the most comprehensive celestial atlas ever published, the first to attempt a complete representation of all 15,000 naked-eye stars. Particularly striking is the number of unformed stars, that is those lying outside any constellation. It was in order to catalogue these satisfactorily that Bode proposed the novel step of designating constellation boundaries, effectively defining regions of the sky. This system was to become fundamental to astronomy, although the fixing of the boundaries occupied many years experiment and adjustment.

the pointed crown of his Cepheus shows traces of Islamic influence. A few decades later Johannes Honter has adopted a thoroughly vernacular style, his male figures dressed for a northern winter like German merchants or courtiers. Elements of this vernacular or contemporary style re-appear throughout the seventeenth century; Boötes for example was always likely to be depicted as a northern hunter with boots and furs, while Cepheus somehow became cast as an oriental king rather than a Hellenic one. But on the whole most mapmakers aimed at a more or less classical style, the globes of Blaeu and the *Uranometria* figures of Bayer forming the most widely imitated models. Certain mythological attributes of the characters which are not strictly derived from the star patterns tend to be emphasized in this tradition, such as Hercules's lion-skin, Perseus's winged shoes, or Andromeda's chains. These were elements which had appeared constantly in the much older pictorial tradition of the Aratus-Hyginus manuscripts. They were evidently the visual badges of those characters, and irrespective of any scientific significance, the wider, classically-educated public expected to see them. This self-conscious classicism is not found of course in star charts from beyond Europe. Celestial maps continued to be drawn in Islamic countries down to the nineteenth century, and artists in India for example had no inhibitions about employing a lively vernacular style in their constellation figures.

The rich flowering of celestial maps as a published genre between 1500 and 1800

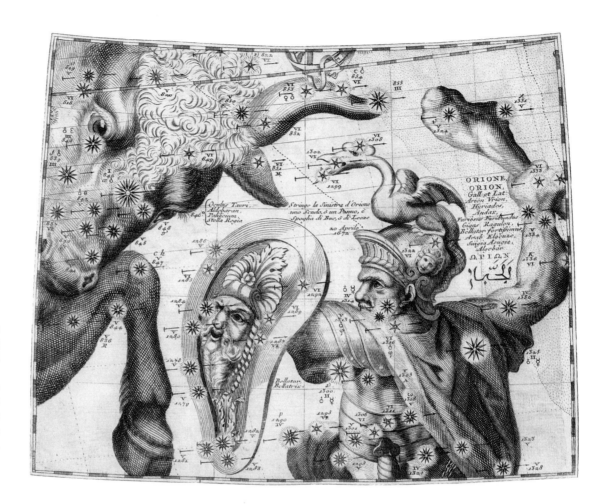

CORONELLI: ORION AND TAURUS, *c.*1701. The Venetian Vincenzo Coronelli brought the craft of globe-making to its height, producing unique hand-painted models for individual patrons, as well as printing globe-gores. Although impeccably scientifically based (the inclusion of Arabic names is most unusual) the main object of these richly engraved artefacts was frankly artistic: the positions of the stars are almost lost in the superbly sculptured forms of the constellations.
The British Library, C.6.d.9

raises the question of why the star chart should have emerged and flourished in this period. The answers appear to have less to do with any scientific breakthrough than with the broader changes in thought and society at the time. The most obvious and far-reaching cultural event at the opening of this period was the impact of printing, the consequent spread of literacy and the way in which these two forces together began to erode the oral and traditional transmission of skills and knowledge. For centuries astronomers, astrologers, calendar-makers and navigators had received their knowledge of the stars from their teachers, and much of their lore was learned by rote, indeed part of their professional craft lay in their use of the art of memory. In the same way the poet, the physician, the priest or the musician held in his mind the canons and secrets of his art. The spread of printing began to change all that, first by offering to anyone who cared to read instant access to the accumulated material of centuries in any field from algebra

INDIAN STAR CHART, *c.*1840. The classical constellations and the science of Ptolemy had become deeply-rooted in India, both Muslim and Hindu India, while astronomy since the scientific revolution was ignored. Manuscript star charts such as this continued to be produced until the late nineteenth century, showing a lively vernacular style. The southern constellations, which had begun to appear on western star maps around the year 1600, were not incorporated into these traditional documents, whose main function was still astrological.

The British Library, O.I.O.C. Or. 5259, ff,56v–7

THOMAS WRIGHT: THE COSMOS, 1750. Wright, an instrument-maker and amateur astronomer, was perhaps the first man to attempt to rationalize the large-scale structure of the cosmos. The Copernican revolution and the invention of the telescope both combined to produce a perception of a much vaster universe. Wright speculated that it might be infinite, that the sky visible from the earth, with its concentration of stars in the Milky Way, might be a discrete system, and that such systems might be replicated throughout the universe. Although Wright's ideas were not empirically based, they were in some senses prophetic.

The British Library, 49.e.15

to zoology; and secondly by fostering the sense that all knowledge *must* be written down, published and disseminated. The elite, or arcane, personally-transmitted knowledge was becoming a thing of the past. In the century from 1470–1570 all the foundation texts of western science, philosophy, and literature were taken out of the elite manuscript collections and offered in print in the market places of Europe. And this applied not only to texts: at the same time there was a quickening of the visual imagination, which demanded that the natural and human world be analyzed and presented in diagrams and images. Anatomy, architecture, mechanics, and geography were all presented in early printed works enriched with seminal illustrations. This innovation coincided with a further force at work in Renaissance thought — the revival of classical models. The overwhelming motive behind the visual art of the sixteenth and seventeenth centuries was to rival or surpass the art of antiquity. The classical constellations were seen as a direct visual link with the science and the imagination of the Greeks and Romans. Their reproduction and dissemination gave an opportunity for educated people to affirm their classical inheritance. The star chart was a small-scale expression of the vogue for classical models, just as the Palladian villa was a large-scale one.

But beneath these facets of intellectual history there was a yet deeper, religious,

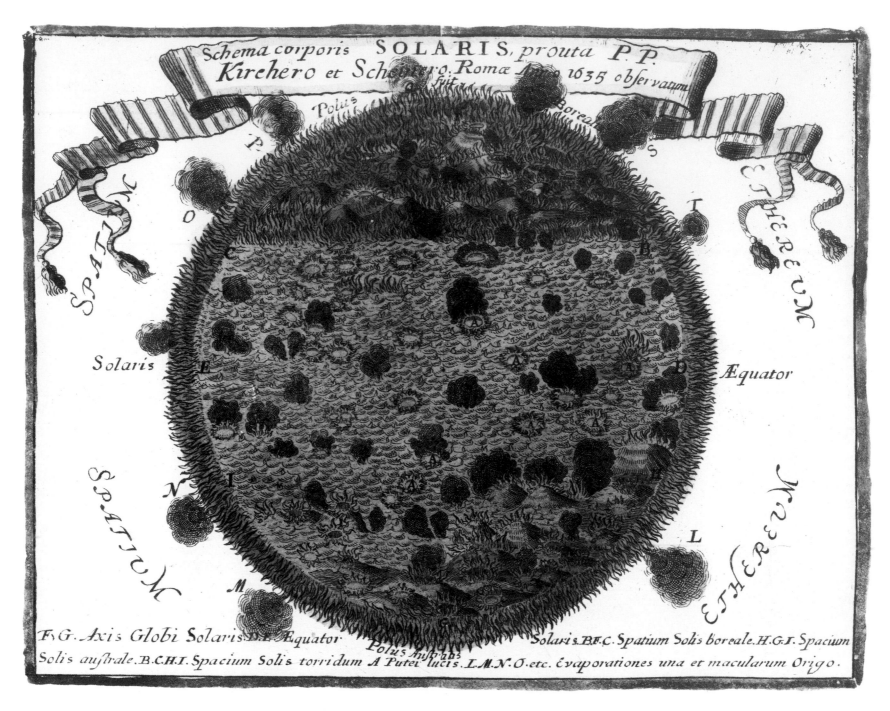

Schema corporis **SOLARIS,** prouta P.P.
Kirchero et Scheinero Romæ Anno 1635 observatum

Polus Borealis

SPATIUM

ÆTHEREUM

Solaris

Æquator

SPATIUM

ÆTHEREUM

F.G. Axis Globi Solaris D.E. Æquator *Solaris. B.F.C. Spatium Solis boreale. H.G.I. Spacium*
Polus Australis
Solis australe. B.C.H.I. Spacium Solis torridum A Putei lucis. L.M.N.O. etc. Evaporationes una et macularum Origo.

MAP OF THE SUN from Seller's *Atlas Coelestis*, 1680. From an early date the telescope was used to project images of the sun, although their interpretation was highly speculative. Mountains, volcanoes and clouds were supposed to exist on the surface, and it was even considered possible that the sun was inhabited.
The British Library, Maps 1.aa.46

motive which focused the mind on astronomy and its images. This was what later in the eighteenth century came to be called Natural Theology, the attempt to explain the workings of the cosmos as a guide to the divine will and purpose. It is striking that many of the greatest astronomers, such as Kepler and Newton, were deeply religious men, consciously seeking to lay bare the laws of cosmic harmony by which, they were convinced, God sustained the universe. One of the earliest texts of this new Natural Theology was William Derham's *Astro-Theology, or a Demonstration of the Being and Attributes of God from a Survey of the Heavens*, which went through ten editions in the fifty years following its appearance in 1715. Derham describes the 'new system' of astronomy, that is the Newtonian, as the 'most rational and probable because it is far the most magnificent of any; and worthy of an infinite Creator'. He spends much time speculating

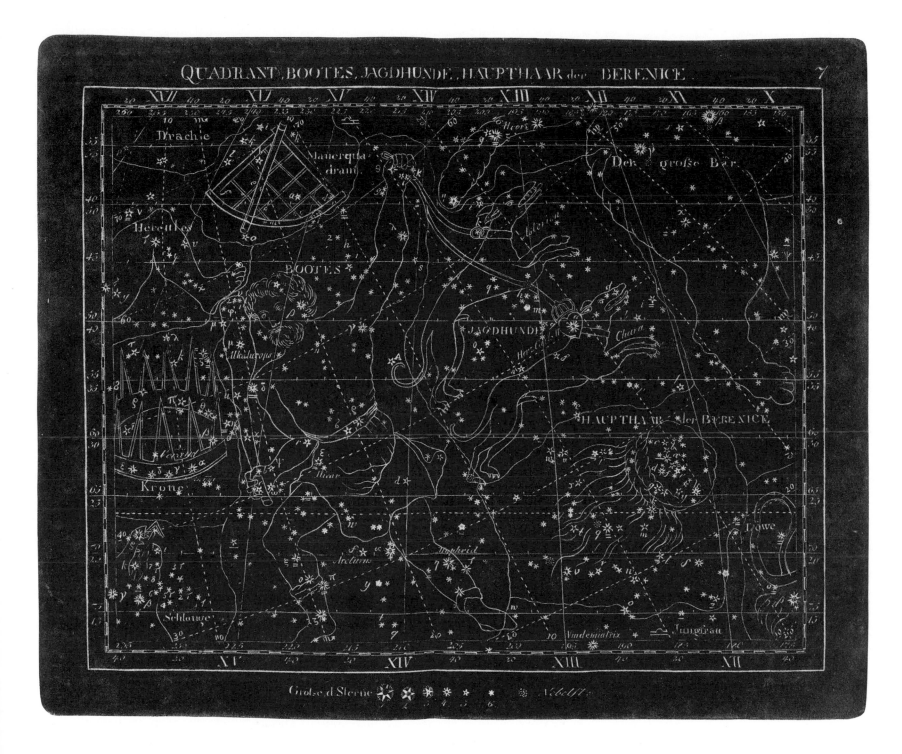

GOLDBACH STAR CHART, 1803. All star charts down to this time had been conventionally printed as black engraved lines on white paper. The novel idea of imitating the night sky more correctly by printing the stars white on a black background led to a nineteenth century vogue for these more naturalistic sky maps.
The British Library, Maps 7.aa.1

that 'Every fixt star is a sun and encompassed with a system of planets', and that these planets are probably inhabited. The creation of a plurality of worlds is presented as a rational occupation for an omnipotent deity. Derham's entire book is an extended argument for the magnificence of God deduced from that of his creation, and is expressed in purely rational terms. The eclipse of astrology and of theories of celestial influence is total. From the same rationalizing impulse as Derham's work came a novel form of solar system map in three dimensions, the Orrery, the ingenious clockwork model of the planets circling the sun. The planets' sizes and distances could not be shown in scale of course, but the periods of their revolutions were, and the more elaborate models included their satellites too. The eighteenth-century delight in celestial mechanics could scarcely have taken a more palpable form than this intellectual toy.

As in the thought of the eighteenth century, so in its images: in the ever-clearer and more complete sky-maps of this period from Bayer to Bode, we seem to detect a process of *demystification* of the heavens, a process of elucidating the riddles of the universe, and placing them within the grasp of rational human thought. Support for this interpretation appears in one of the most curious astronomical thinkers of the eighteenth century, Thomas Wright, whose *Original Theory or New Hypothesis of the Universe*, 1750 influenced no less a figure than Immanuel Kant. Wright turned from locational star mapping to constructing graphic models of the very structure of the universe, grappling with the distribution of stars, the possible existence of other galaxies, and the idea of a necessary divine centre of the universe. As the vastness of space became evident during the eighteenth century, Wright mused that 'the endless Immensity is an unlimited Plenum of Creations not unlike the known Universe', which was sustained by 'an infinite all-active Power'. Is it too much to suggest that in their desire to chart the heavens, the celestial mapmakers of the seventeenth and eighteenth centuries were actually charting man's place within the universe? Confident in the clock-like mechanism of the cosmos, the astronomer sought in the changeless realm of the stars, if it could be measured and understood, a key to the divine mind. The chains of being which had been sought by astrology had receded into the past by the seventeenth century, to be replaced by a scientific quest for the mechanical force which held the universe in equilibrium. The mapping of the heavens, which flourished in a particular form during the formative years of modern science, may be seen as a small but significant expression of a theistic school of natural philosophy. Thus the links between astronomy and religion, observation and divination, which were so strong in the most ancient cultures, and which were so theologically important during the middle ages, remained still unbroken in the age of science.

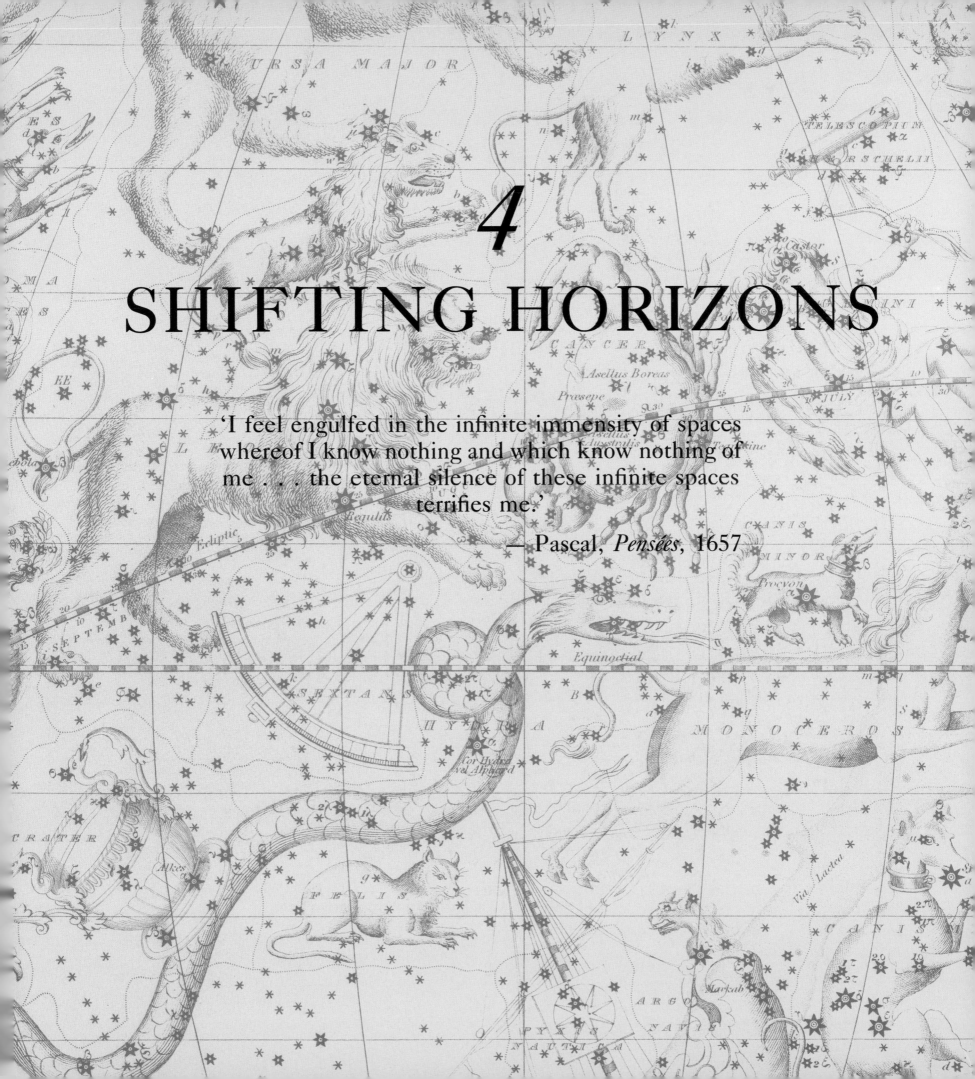

4
SHIFTING HORIZONS

'I feel engulfed in the infinite immensity of spaces whereof I know nothing and which know nothing of me . . . the eternal silence of these infinite spaces terrifies me.'

— Pascal, *Pensées*, 1657

AND ATELIER TYPOGRAPHIQUE.

W HEN JUDGED BY ITS ASTRONOMY, the eighteenth century deserves its reputation as an era of light. Newton's physics was accepted by scientists and theologians as offering a deeply satisfying vision of nature and its creator. Yet the focus of Newtonian celestial mechanics was very much on the solar system. Beyond the paths of the planets was a farther and more mysterious dimension, for the nature of the stars and the structure of the stellar universe were still hidden. By common consent, modern cosmology began two centuries ago with the work of William Herschel, but despite many startling breakthroughs, no second Newton has appeared to flood our eyes with light. On the contrary we seem to advance through a tortuous maze in which no map can aid us. In this period of astronomy, a new visual dimension has been added through space photography, and the *mapping* of the heavens has arguably given way to the *image* of the heavens. In the shaping of modern cosmology, the interaction of thought and image has had enormous consequences for the professional astronomer, and has assumed a dominant role in the popular mind.

William Herschel (1738–1822) achieved fame as the discoverer of Uranus in 1781, becoming the first man since the dawn of classical astronomy to enlarge the bounds of the solar system. His discovery came in the course of a monumental new sky survey in which he was engaged, with no less an object than to lay bare the structure of the universe, to see beyond the flat surface of the starry sphere and grasp its three-dimensional form. The locations of the stars as observed by Ptolemy or Tycho or Flamsteed were expressed in terms of angular measurement, and this information lay behind the traditional two-dimensional star chart. Even the celestial globe, although it is a three-dimensional object, actually shows the sky only as a surface, in two dimensions. By the late eighteenth century the desire to penetrate beyond the shell of the starry sphere and gauge the scale of the universe had become urgent. The general view of cosmology in this period, with all its uncertainties, is admirably summed up by Samuel Dunn, a writer on astronomy and geography:

'The number of stars which have been accurately observed is no more than 3,000. Yet by the help of telescopes, 21 stars have been seen in the space which forms the cloudy star (i.e. the nebula) of Orion's sword, 36 in that of the cloudy star of Pegasus, 78 in the asterism of the Pleiades, and 2,000 in the constellation of Orion. From which it has been conjectured that the number of fixed stars is no less than 10 million, beside those of the Via Lactea, or Milky Way, and such as cannot be discerned by the best glasses, and that twice or thrice that number would cover the expanse of Heaven. The bright star Syrius in the constellation of the Great Dog hath been estimated to be distant from us more than 2 million of million miles. And the distance of a star of lesser apparent magnitude hath been found to be more than 30 million of million miles. Wherefore tis concluded that every fixed star is a sun, having planets and comets moving round it like those which move round our sun. From all of which it may be concluded that, if the universe doth not extend itself beyond the powers of number, weight and measure, it may extend too far for human reason to comprehend. Particles of light are inconceivably small, hard bodies thrown off from the sun, stars etc. which move at the rate of 10 million miles in a minute of time and come from the sun to our earth in 8 minutes, and from the fixed stars in about six years.'

It is clear from writers such as Dunn that the problems of cosmological scale were beginning to be understood, even if the answers were remote and mysterious. Herschel's

SAMUEL LEIGH *URANIA'S MIRROR*, 1823. An ingenious novelty typical of its time, these were cards showing the constellations, pierced with holes to mark the star positions. When the card was held against a light, the constellation appeared as in the night sky, an excellent demonstrational or mnemonic device. The printing equipment shown here was one of a number of short-lived constellations with technical subjects proposed by early nineteenth-century astronomers (another was Montgolfier's balloon) mainly to fill areas in the southern sky.
The Royal Astronomical Society, London

novel conception involved estimating the radial distances of stars from the earth. In the classical doctrine of the starry sphere, the stars were conceived to be each of differing brilliance, but all set in one spherical shell located at a specific distance from the earth. This doctrine was weakened and finally shattered by a number of blows. First, in the Copernican system the revolution of the earth should have revealed obvious stellar parallaxes; that it failed to do so suggested the possibility that the stars were at a far greater distance than had been imagined. Second, the actual existence of the starry sphere became impossible in the thought of Tycho, Kepler and their successors. Third, the telescope revealed in any given field of view more stars than had been visible to the naked eye, and the more powerful the instrument the more stars appeared. Finally the very notion of the 'fixed stars' was challenged in 1718 by Edmond Halley's announcement that he had detected small movements ('proper motions') among the stars. Subsequently this movement of the stars was found to be caused partly by the motion through space of the solar system itself, but also to be shared by all stars in their own right. One incidental effect of these movements will be to destroy the constellations as we know them: in a quarter of a million years they will be clearly re-shaped, and in half a million years they would be unrecognizable. All these discoveries had the cumulative effect of suggesting that the stars were *scattered* throughout space at varying radial distances from earth. In this view the different magnitudes of brightness were explicable simply in terms of distance from earth. But given that this was so, was there a structure to the realm of the stars, or was the distribution random? Galileo and the other early telescope users had resolved much of the Milky Way into stars: what was the significance of this concentration of stars?

To decide these questions, to map the universe in three dimensions, it was obviously necessary to know stellar distances; but in the absence of stellar parallaxes, this was precisely what Herschel did not know. He overcame the difficulty by making the assumption that all stars are of similar absolute brilliance and that stellar magnitude was therefore an index of distance from earth. Working on this principle Herschel proposed that the Milky Way held the key to the structure of the universe, that the universe was a disk-shaped mass of stars which we see edge-on as the Milky Way. When we look at right angles to the Milky Way we are seeing through the thinning eges of the disk towards empty space. The tentative model which he published in 1785 shows the sun near the centre of a rather ragged disk. The earlier work of Thomas Wright was purely hypothetical, but this drawing by Herschel marks the dawn of observational cosmology. In fact however, as he built and used more and more powerful instruments (the largest was a 40-foot reflector), his faith in his early theory was shaken, for he perceived that certain of the nebulae, the clouds resembling luminous dust that were far removed from the plane of the Milky Way, were resolvable into myriads of innumerable stars; on his disk-model there should be no high star concentrations at those places. Herschel undertook what was the most ambitious and detailed sky survey made to that date, which involved the counting of hundreds of thousands of stars subdivided within minute fields of view, in order to study patterns of star distribution and concentration. This work did not however lead to new published star charts since that was not its purpose. The problem of understanding the scale of what the observer was seeing would haunt astronomy for a further century and a half. Nor was there yet any key to the internal nature of the stars, for the science of astrophysics had not yet been born. Even a man like Herschel could not envisage how the processes at work in the sun could ever be approached, and he was capable of speculating that the sun was a 'lucid planet' possibly inhabited by men who were protected by thick clouds from its fiery upper atmosphere. The technical advances in chemistry, physics and instrumentation that would bring astronomy into the laboratory lay still in the future, and such speculations

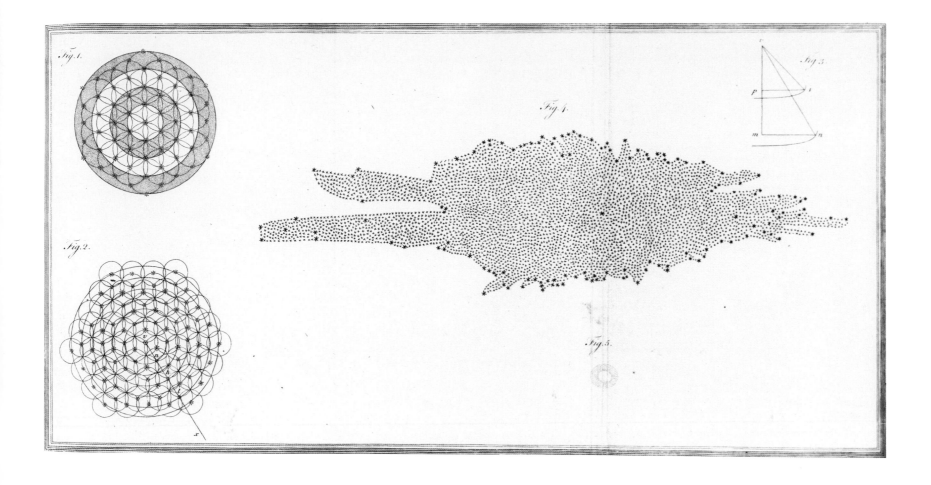

were commonplace even among leading scientists.

Similarly in terms of star mapping, the first half of the nineteenth century does not see any radical break with the past. It is often claimed that Bode's great celestial atlas of 1801 marked the end of the pictorial star chart tradition, but this is not accurate. It is true that no pictorial star atlases more detailed or more elaborate than Bode's were produced, but smaller atlases very much derived from Bode continued to appear throughout the century, some frankly popular but others claiming to be based on original observations, and offering new, practical chart design. It became fashionable to publish star maps, especially monthly or seasonal ones, white on black, to match the appearance of the night sky. When a recognizable skyline — that of London or Paris for example — was drawn at the base of the map, the distinctly artistic illusion was achieved that one was surveying from the comfort of one's study the night sky over Greenwich or Montmartre. Middleton's *Celestial Atlas* of 1843 combined austere white on black seasonal maps with some elegant pictorial charts in the traditional style. A more playful novelty was Samuel Leigh's *Urania's Mirror*, 1823, consisting of a series of constellations printed on cards with pierced holes marking the principal stars; when held up to the lamplight the star patterns sprang clearly into shape.

Leigh's novel innovation was not widely copied. But a new type of popular star map that appeared in the mid-nineteenth century did become permanent — the rotating planisphere. Whether consciously modelled on the astrolabe or not, the planisphere works in a similar way by separating the locating map of the stars from its frame of reference, with this difference — that it is the time of visibility that is separate and movable. Basically a projected map of the northern or southern heavens centred on the

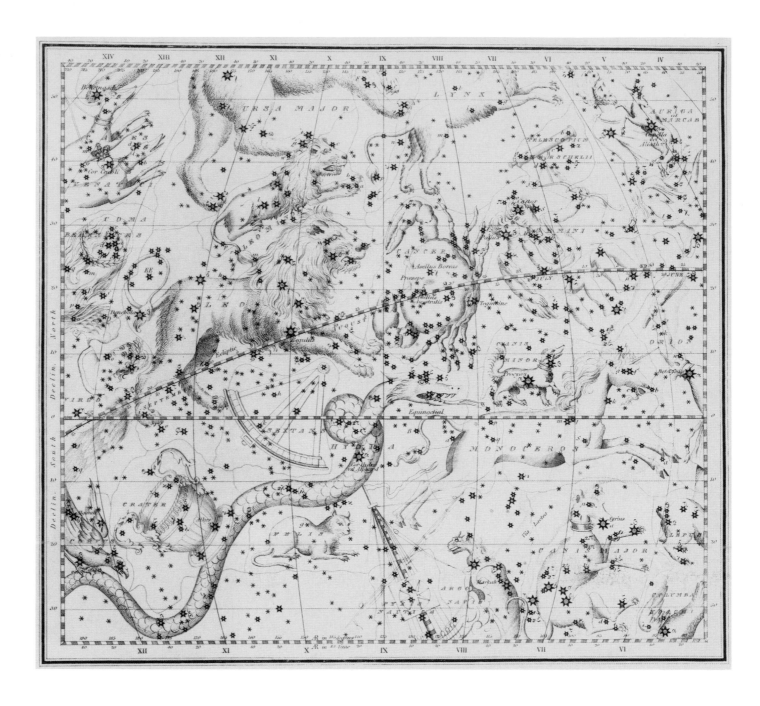

MIDDLETON: *Celestial Atlas*, 1843. By the nineteenth century the pictorial star map had ceased to be used by serious astronomers, but they were still published for the popular market. Middleton's elegant engravings show the constellations in their correct orientation as seen from the earth. They were accompanied by plane charts without the figures to aid observation. The canon of the constellations was by no means fixed at this date: the Telescope shown here had been proposed in honour of Herschel, but it did not become permanent — the southern Telescope is a separate star group. The small cat south of Hydra was another short-lived astronomical caprice.

pole, by masking approximately half of the map the planisphere, shows that part of the sky which is actually visible at any given moment. Like the astrolabe the planisphere is valid only for a given latitude.

Astronomy was promoted in the nineteenth century as a distinctly moral branch of science, one which awakened the mind to religious perception. James Middleton summed up this attitude when he wrote in the preface of his 1843 collection of star charts: 'The man of science may be enabled to discover in the more distant parts of the universe, the same laws and regularities which govern our own system; while the Christian will derive from the science which it teaches, the most sublime illustrations of the wisdom, power and majesty of that Being who garnished the heavens, who telleth the number of the stars, and calleth them all by name.' The perceived conflict between science and religion was to centre on geology and biology, while astronomy, however

SPRING.

MIDDLETON: *Celestial Atlas*, 1843.

challenging its findings might be, always inhabited an ethereal realm which was not felt to be at odds with the religious sensibility.

Far removed from popular astronomy, however, a new style of scientific star map was taking shape. In the first place, the research scientist had no need of the traditional constellation figures, which were a distraction on a serious map. But more important, even the best of the traditional star atlases — that of Bode — showed only some 15,000 stars, the vast majority being naked-eye stars, while the astronomer of the mid-nineteenth century was handling telescopic observations of ten times that number. This situation was comparable perhaps to a pioneer Alpinist planning his climbs with the aid of a map of the whole of Switzerland. To rectify this situation Friedrich Argelander published in Bonn his *Atlas des Nordlichen Gestirnten Himmels*, 1863, commonly referred to as the 'Bonner Durchmusterung' (Bonn Survey), which showed a staggering total of

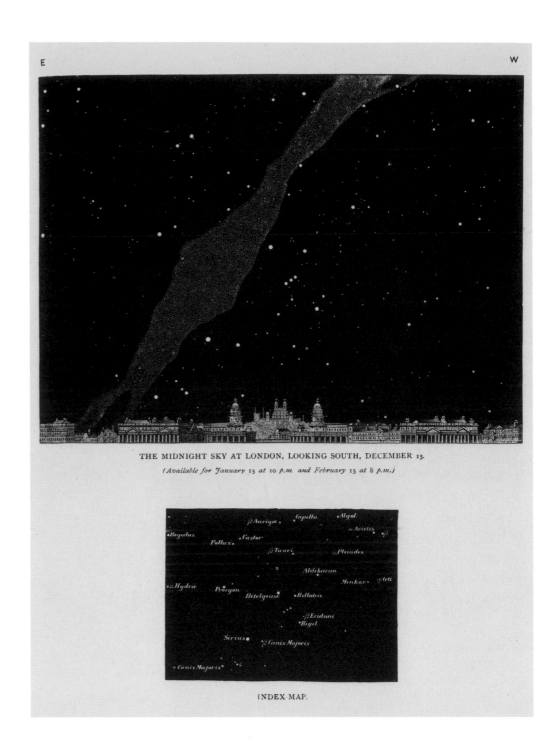

THE MIDNIGHT SKY AT LONDON, LOOKING SOUTH, DECEMBER 15.

(Available for January 15 at 10 p.m. and February 15 at 8 p.m.)

INDEX·MAP.

EDWIN DUNKIN: Winter Sky Over Greenwich, 1879. One of a series of star maps drawn white on black over a recognizable horizon. In their naturalistic approach they cross the boundary from map to picture, even to illusion. This effect has been imitated in the modern planetarium. The clarity of these charts is exemplary, and they were well received by an educated, popular market.
The British Library, 8563.i.3

324,189 stars. As a work of meticulous observation and draftsmanship, it commands our amazed admiration, tempered perhaps with regret that its austere cartography represents the final act in the demystification of the heavens. Initially covering only the northern hemisphere, it was extended by Argelander himself to a declination of −23 degrees by 1886, and by a different team working in Argentina to −62 degrees in 1908, finally mapping the south polar stars in 1930. The accompanying Bonner Durchmusterung star catalogue was for over half a century the internationally recognized celestial reference system. The Bonner Durchmusterung atlas shows no constellations. Argelander had earlier published a very different atlas, the *Uranometria Nova* of 1843, one of whose aims

PLANISPHERE. The revolving planisphere is the most practical form of star chart ever designed: by masking off part of a map of the entire hemisphere, it is able to represent sections of the sky actually visible to the observer. The hours of the night and the days of the year are calibrated around the edge of the disk, so that its rotation mirrors that of the earth itself. It has affinities with the clock and with the astrolabe, from which in turn the clock evolved.

National Maritime Museum, London

was to define a fixed canon of the constellations and to introduce recognized boundary lines between them. Serious astronomers were seeking to rationalize and clarify the map of the heavens; one of the last innovations among the constellations was the division of the very large southern Ship into four — Vela the Sail, Pyxis the Compass, Puppis the Stern, and Carina the Keel. In practice there was no change to the constellations after the middle of the nineteenth century, although the definitive modern list of 88 was not officially endorsed until 1930 under the authority of the International Astronomical Union. This has not of course prevented occasional polemical suggestions for a new sky order, such as that of A. P. Herbert. Herbert's rationalized map of the heavens is perhaps the kind of scheme which the revolutionary government of France might have promoted in the 1790s following its rational calendar reform, if it had not been too busy executing its scientists.

THE PHOTOGRAPHIC REVOLUTION

Argelander's work was particularly impressive for its base in telescopic observation and its use of conventional plotting. Yet it coincided exactly with the first astronomical use of photography, which was to revolutionize many of the methods and the fundamental

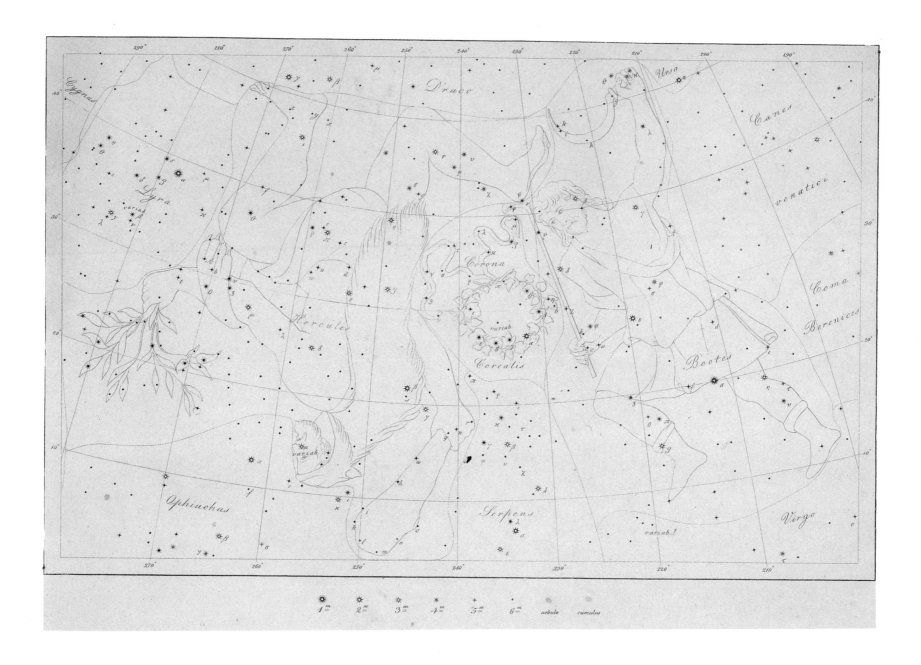

ARGELANDER'S PROGRESS. In 1843 Friedrich Argelander published *Uranometria Nova*,
an unrevolutionary celestial atlas, showing the
traditional constellation figures and tentative
boundaries between constellation-sectors. He
was soon to begin work an epoch-making sky
survey resulting in a new type of star map for
a new age of rigorous astronomy. The *Atlas des
Nordlichen Gestirnten Himmels* of 1863 showed
no constellations, no boundaries, no names, no
symbols of any kind, merely an austere
monochrome fabric composed of 324,189 stars.
Even though it reached initially only to −2
degrees, each page showed many thousands of
stars. Based entirely on optical sightings, Argelander's work was the last monument of the
pre-photographic age of star mapping.

The British Library, 14000.c.42 and Maps 24.e.5

concepts of astronomy. Beginning in the 1850s the moon and the sun were naturally the
first objects to be photographed, followed by the most photogenic planets, Saturn and
Jupiter. It was inevitable that the new technique would make an enormous impact on
star mapping, for two principal reasons: the time-exposed photographic plate could
detect light-sources far fainter than the human eye, and it could preserve the image for
later study and analysis. In 1887 a conference in Paris initiated a vast international astro-
photography programme with the aim of publishing a new *Carte du Ciel*, which would be
an atlas not of redrawn maps, but of photographic prints, complete with added co-
ordinates. Very much in the organisers' minds were the recent pictures by the French
brothers Prosper and Paul Henry of the Pleiades, which showed more than 1,000 stars
compared with less than 100 detectable even with a good telescope. Due to organizatio-
nal problems, this programme dragged on for 80 years, while other more tightly-focused
projects overtook it. One such, which resulted not in published maps but in a vast
catalogue of the southern stars, was the *Cape Photographic Durchmusterung* which Jacob

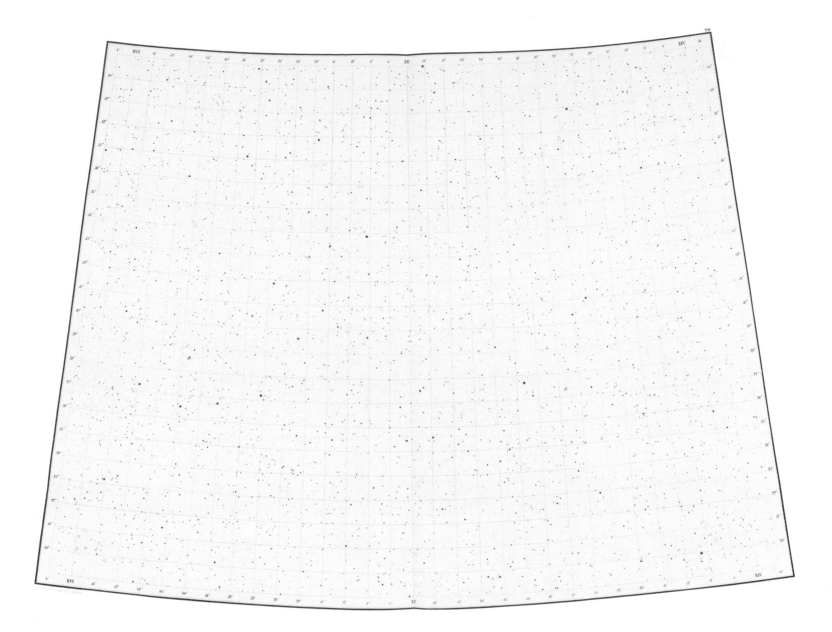

Kapteyn produced between 1896 and 1900. Working in a laboratory in Groningen, Kapteyn used a series of photographic plates from the Cape Observatory to measure the co-ordinates of 454,875 stars between declination −18 and the south pole, down to the tenth magnitude. This desire for absolute precision and completeness was of course an ever-receding mirage, since improving astro-photography would always bring more and more stars into view. The summit of this type of photography was reached with the National Geographic-Palomar Observatory Sky Survey of 1954–58. A series of 1,758 plates, each showing thousands of stars reaching down to magnitude 21, it expanded the published image of the universe by 25 times. It carried the observer across a billion light years of space and its stars are as uncountable as those in the sky itself.

Scarcely less important was the new technique of spectroscopy, developed in 1860 by Kirchhoff and Bunsen. It had always been thought that no direct knowledge of the composition of the sun and stars would ever be possible. The discovery that the analysis of light revealed in detail the chemical and physical characters of the light source proved

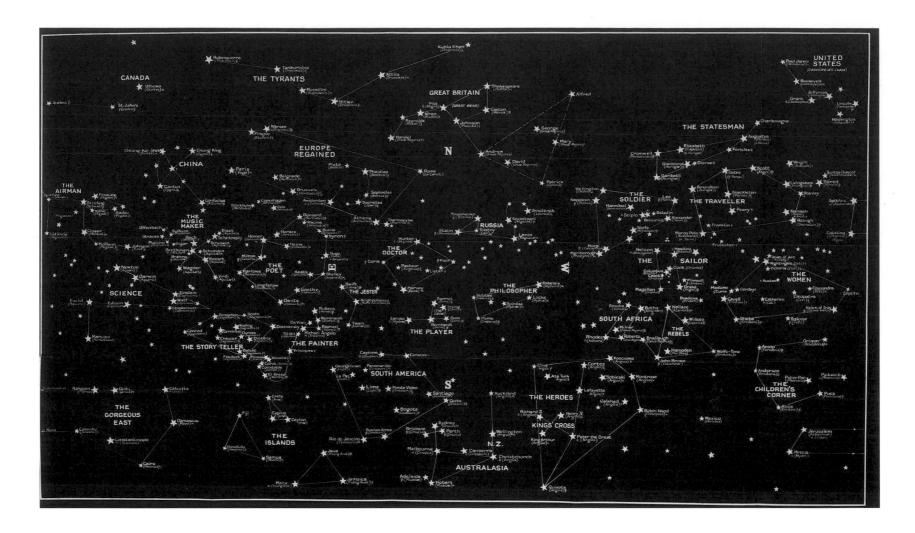

A. P. HERBERT: *A Better Sky*, 1944. Herbert started from the premise that we know or care little for astronomy and the stars because their mythology and their names are alien to us. He proposed a reformed, rational sky rooted in modern experience. He renamed the constellations and all the principal stars. Ursa Major became Great Britain, with Shakespeare, Wren and Johnson as the stars: Draco became the Tyrants, composed of Robespierre, Hitler and Mussolini; Cassiopeia was transformed into the United States with Washington, Jefferson and Lincoln; Orion, with the stars Columbus, Cook and Nelson became the Sailor. Sadly for Herbert, his reformed astronomy shared the fate of all other similar projects.

the foundation of astrophysics, and later of the processes of evolution in the universe. Working with stellar spectra just a few years later in 1868, the English astronomer William Huggins made a discovery that was to assume the first importance in modern cosmology. Analyzing the light emitted by the star Sirius, he found that its spectrum was shifting markedly to the red. This phenomenon had been theoretically described in general terms by the Austrian physicist Christian Doppler, as an effect of the changing wavelength of a moving energy source — it applies to sound as well as light. Huggins's calculations indicated that Sirius was moving away from the earth, at a velocity of around 100,000 mph. The full implications of this effect would become clearer half a century later, when related findings would be gathered from distant galaxies.

By accident, the discovery of spectroscopy coincided with the invention of colour printing in the 1860s. It had always been known that stars shone with many different colours — Ptolemy had spoken of 'golden-red Arcturus' — but these colours could now be mass-produced and offered to a wide public. In time their scientific significance would become clearer, and it was in the mid-1950s that the Czech astronomer Antonin Becvar pioneered the use of colour and symbol in published star maps to indicate a wide variety of analyzed information about the stars. The star atlases of today, both those for the professional and for the amateur sky-watcher, do more than locate positions for they are able to draw on the results of spectroscopy and photography. They may show the spectral class and magnitude of the stars, and whether they are multiple or variable, as well as non-stellar objects such as galaxies, nebulae, clusters and gas-clouds. The mapping of the heavens has now progressed beyond the locational, which has become the province of photography, while redrawn maps may be used to display levels of thematic information derived from wider analysis.

The excitement of photography was just one of the reasons behind a new genre of popular astronomy books which proliferated in the later nineteenth century. Proctor and Dunkin in England, Guillemin and Flammarion in France, produced summaries of the latest findings illustrated with pioneering photographs of eclipses, of the rings of Saturn, and, before the end of the century, of the nebulae that were increasingly engaging the attention of astronomers. In this period the dividing line between what could be achieved

GUILLEMIN: The Night Sky over Paris, 1865. Probably the inspiration behind Dunkin's similar maps over the London skyline. Guillemin has drawn the architecture of Paris with great care to create an illusionistic effect.
The British Library, 8560.g.27

LE CIEL DE L'HORIZON DE PARIS (Côté Sud)

Left: ISAAC ROBERTS: Orion Nebula, 1889. In the late nineteenth century astro-photography revolutionized astronomy in two ways: a time-exposed film could capture more light-sources than the human eye even when the eye was aided by a telescope; and it could preserve the image for future analysis. Isaac Roberts was one of a number of amateur enthusiasts who pioneered astro-photography, in particular in devising the essential clock-driven mounting which held the camers's field of view. This picture was exposed for 3½ hours. The study of nebula photographs was to assume ever-greater importance in modern cosmology.

The British Library, 8563.i.24

Right: AMADÉ GUILLEMIN: The Colour of the Stars, 1865. In the 1860s the new technique of spectroscopy revolutionized astrophysics by revealing the chemistry within stars, a subject which a few years earlier had been felt to be quite out of reach. By accident, it coincided exactly with the advent of colour printing, and spectral analyses such as this one became readily communicable both to the scientific and the non-specialist public. It had always been noticed that certain stars shone red, others, some yellow and others blue: with the technique of spectroscopy, it was understood that these colours revealed the age and nature of the stars.

The British Library, 8560.g.27

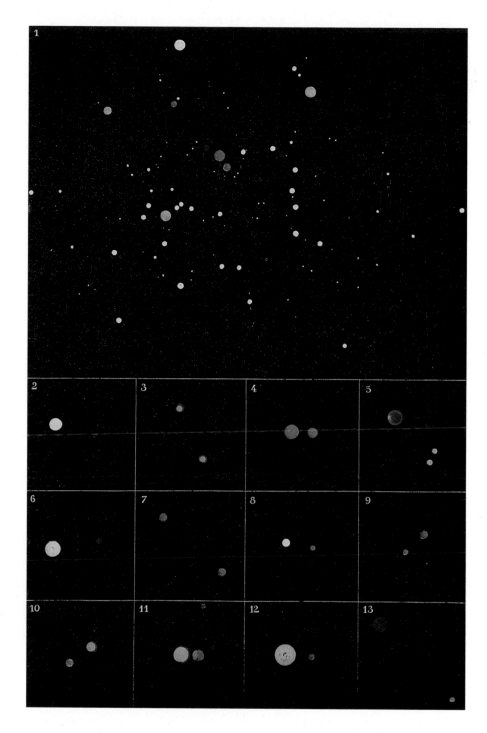

by professional and amateur astronomers was by no means fixed, and landmark discoveries and photographs could be made by amateurs such as Norman Lockyer, who identified helium in the sun, and Henry Draper in New York, who took the first photograph of the Orion nebula in 1880. The many high-quality photographs by Isaac Roberts became features in astronomical books and journals between 1890 and 1920. Part of the excitement of astro-photography was undoubtedly the ambiguity of some of the new features it revealed. Intense interest in the possibility of life on Mars was aroused by the interpretative drawings based on photographs by Lowell and Schiaparelli. The books of Camille Flammarion in particular, one of the great nineteenth-century popularizers, are a heady mixture of science and imagination, photography and fantasy.

Photography and spectroscopy placed powerful new tools in the hands of astronomers, and the secular development of physics and chemistry prepared the ground for a new phase of modern cosmology, in which the problems of scale and structure in the universe were determinedly addressed. It was the interpretation of nebulae which proved to be decisive. Some of the great nebulae are visible to the naked eye and Ptolemy had described half a dozen, including the Andromeda nebula, as 'misty, cloud-like stars'. Their luminosity was no different from that of a normal star, and on the luminosity-distance principle they must be part of the familiar star system, just as Sirius or Antares or any other star was, although they clearly differed in some way from those other stars. Herschel's observations with his largest telescope however raised the problem that some nebulae appeared to be actually composed of stars. This was an isolated problem to which there was no answer, and even in 1885 the Andromeda nebula was thought to be some type of nova remnant, situated perhaps 30,000 light years away — a vast enough distance but well within the bounds of our star system. The real difficulty came in the early twentieth century when ever-improving instruments and photographs resolved this nebula and most others into what were unmistakably discrete systems of stars in their

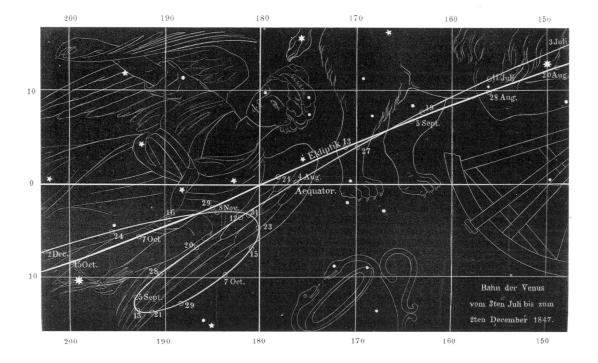

JOHANN MÜLLER: Path of the Planet Venus, 1847. A long-standing problem with star charts was their unsuitability to show planetary and lunar positions. Because they are in motion against the background of stars, their positions would necessarily appear as lines which would tend to dominate the map. More important, their irregular paths means that any map would be valid for a few months only — a decisive factor for the commercial map publisher. Planetary positions were published in textual form as 'ephemerides'. Müller's map is an interesting example map of a planet's position made for purely demonstrational purposes in a scientific textbook.

The British Library, 8710.b.1

own right. It was Edwin Hubble who, working from the known properties of certain variable stars found in the Andromeda nebula, was able to calculate its distance as approaching a breathtaking one million light years (and this figure was subsequently doubled). The conclusion became irresistible that this was a star system paralleling our own Milky Way, and vastly distanced from it. It was at this stage, the 1920s, that the word galaxy assumed its modern meaning. The word nebula has remained in use, and some of them are indeed clouds of gas; but the majority are more correctly described as galaxies, vast but discreet star groups like our own, comparable to islands in the ocean of space.

No less spectacular and disturbing was Hubble's confirmation of certain earlier

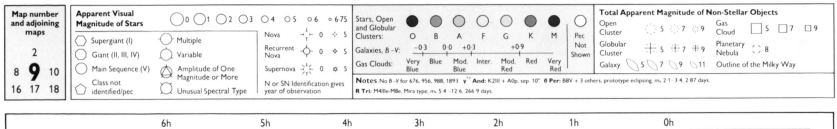

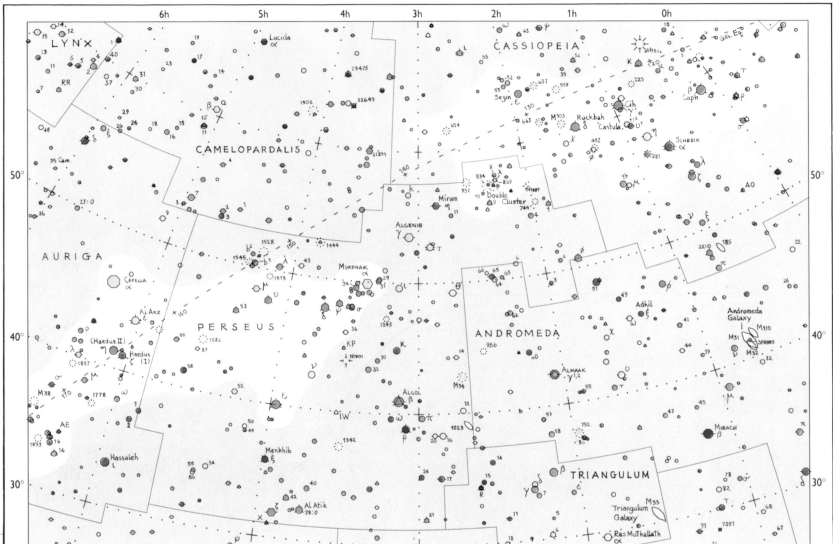

COLOUR STAR ATLAS, 1991, by Cox and Monkhouse. Modern star maps have progressed beyond simply locating the stars: they now show spectral and structural characteristics through the use of colour and symbol. Notice for example the red giant star Almaak in Adromeda, which is also shown to be a multiple, and note the unmistakable symbol for galaxies. The Supernova in Cassiopeia is that observed by Tycho in 1572. The geometric constellations boundaries are an essential feature of modern star catalogues and maps.

Courtesy: George Philip Publishers

findings that in the light from these distant nebulae, certain features were shifted decisively to the red end of the spectrum, which is the characteristic sign of a receding energy source. Hubble was able to show that this recessional velocity was proportional to the distance from earth: the further away these galaxies were, the faster they were travelling. The velocity of these distant galaxies was staggering, measured in thousands of miles per second, and such recession was observable in every part of the universe. The scale of the universe, and its state of dynamic growth, have been discoveries as revolutionary to the modern mind as the Copernican theory was in the sixteenth century. Their implications seem to take us to the limits of human thought, not least in the way that they fuse space and time together. As early as 1676 the Danish astronomer Rømer had demonstrated that light travels at a finite speed, but the full implications of that fact in the field of cosmology emerged only as the true scale of the universe came to be appreciated. Modern instruments can now 'see' some twelve billion light years into space. But of course what is seen is the received light which left its source twelve billion years ago. So in looking across the universe like this, we see a cross-section of time, of the history of the universe, as well as space. There is no limit to the universe, only a 'cosmic event horizon' which we can never cross because light itself defines it, and light

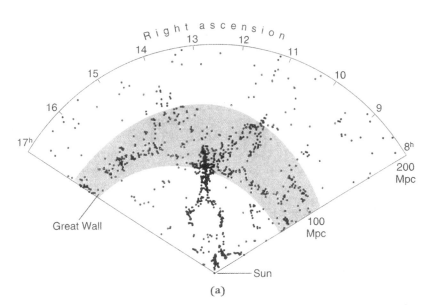

(a)

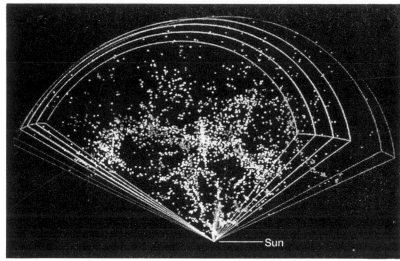

THE DISTRIBUTION OF GALAXIES. (a) Distances of galaxies plotted in a narrow section of sky between 27 degrees and 32 degrees. The radial distance from the solar system is approximately 650 million light years. The viewpoint is directly comparable to that of the classical star chart — from an imaginary point above the north pole. The stick-like human figure is strikingly evident. (b) Similar plots for four adjacent latitudes are superimposed, reinforcing the initial pattern. These small diagrams are probably the most ambitious stellar maps ever conceived.

Smithsonian Center for Astrophysics

can never be overtaken. It is no accident that the age of the universe is also conceived to be of the order of twelve billion years, since that is the time the universe has taken to arrive at its perceived extent: whether the scale is one of time or space, the figure is the same. Quasars for example are observed to be in the most distant regions of the universe; they are considered to have evolved comparatively soon after the birth of the universe, and to be the nucleus of some types of galaxy. Hence the correlation between time and distance is clear: in looking across the universe to distant quasars we are looking back to embryonic galaxies which no longer exist in that form. We are invited to conceive of a universe that is in some way finite in space and time, but whose extent can never be measured even in theory. We may feel free to doubt whether these paradoxes are truly objective, physical realities, or will prove to be categories of human thought and perception. The paradox of the universe's endless growth through unimaginable levels of energy change is captured in the evocative phrase 'catastrophic evolution'.

The contemporary perception of a universe of transcendent mystery has been fed by a new generation of dramatic astronomical photographs whose appeal is both aesthetic and intellectual. We now see across billions of miles of space to multicolored nebulae, galaxies, interstellar dust and supernovae, as an earlier generation once delighted in images of sunrise, storm-clouds and mountains. As celestial maps have become evermore austere and functional, so the art of the astro-photographer has become more lavish and kaleidoscopic; the taste for visual drama which was once satisfied by the mythology of the constellations has been transferred from maps to photographs. Strictly speaking this is not photography but electronic imaging using the charge-coupled device, whose photo-sensitivity is vastly superior to chemical film. Processing allows considerable enhancement of the subjects, and the results are often breathtaking. They represent

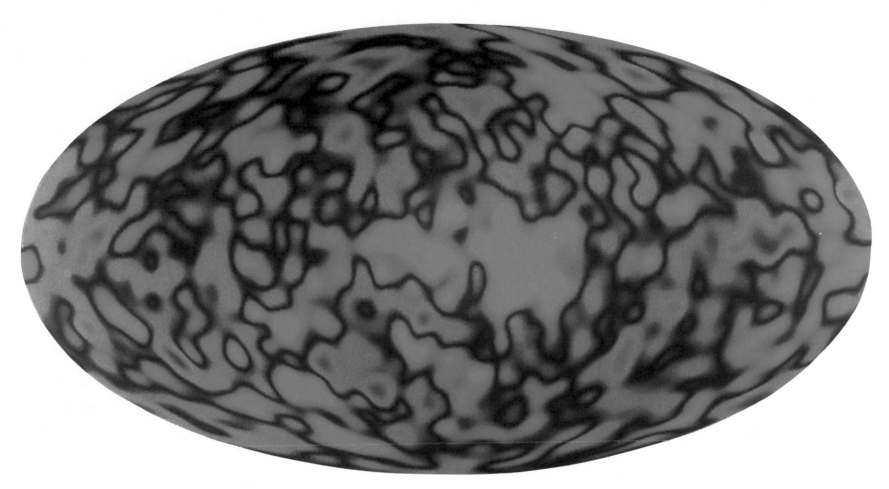

COSMIC RADIATION. Data collected from the Cosmic Background Explorer satellite shows temperature fluctuations in cosmic radiation. This is claimed to relate to the uneven distribution of matter in the universe, and to be comparable to physical ripples or echoes of the Big Bang with which the universe began.
NASA/Science Photo Library

HERTZSPRUNG-RUSSELL DIAGRAM. Evolved independently during the years 1908–1913 by the Dane Ejnar Hertzsprung and the American H. N. Russell, the diagram relates absolute magnitudes with spectral class. The seven spectral types are coded conventionally BAFGKMN in diminishing order of temperture. On the lower right are stars of low temperature and low luminosity, progressing in orderly fashion towards the upper left. A distinct class of stars are cool (and therefore red) but very bright — the red giants. Opposite them at lower left are the small, hot stars — white dwarfs. It was understood that the diagram embodies the evolution of stars, from intense heat and light to eventual inactivity and oblivion.

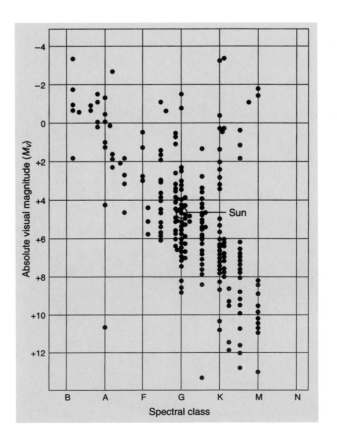

TARANTULA NEBULA. Situated in the Large Magellanic Cloud, in the constellation Dorado, the Tarantula is a vast galaxy, almost one thousand light years in diameter. The Supernova glowing at the bottom right exploded spectacularly on 24 February 1987, when it became visible to the naked eye despite being 150,000 light years away.
Royal Observatory, Edinburgh/Science Photo Library

SPIRAL GALAXY. Number 33 in the Messier catalogue, this is a classic spiral-shaped galaxy in the constellation Triangulum. Its dimension is large — one degree — so that it is just visible to the naked eye.
Dr. Jean Lorre/Science Photo Library

worlds the human eye will never see, whose reality we take on trust from scientists, as once descriptions of heaven were taken on trust from prophets or priests. These images have undoubtedly been used to reinforce a new secular mysticism that seems to surround current cosmology, purveyed in works with titles such as 'Physics and the Mind of God', or 'The Afterglow of Creation', or 'The Search for the Infinite'. From the seventeenth century onwards, Newtonian physics was widely seen as promoting a mechanistic view of the universe in which the image of the clock was used repeatedly. This was not irreligious but it was used to underpin a Christianity that was consciously rational and self-satisfied. The mapmakers of this period were undoubtedly part of this process of demystification. The twentieth-century realization of the unimagined vastness and dynamic movement of the universe have re-awakened a profound sense of mystery, almost of dislocation, in human thought. The placing of astronomy within a religious framework is, as this book has tried to show, a deep-rooted tradition, but it is perhaps surprising that in this secular age the language of physics should reach back to and revive the language of mysticism. In popularizing this kind of thinking, the map of the heavens has been replaced by the image of the heavens, presented in the form our age demands. Perhaps the nearest direct approach to metaphysics in modern astronomy is the discussion of an 'anthropic principle': the fact that the universe is, at any level, comprehensible to the human intellect is thought to indicate a special affinity between man and the cosmos. In its extreme form the anthropic principle even suggests that the purpose of the universe is somehow connected with man, that without man's perception of it, it would have no objective reality. This sets up unmistakable echoes of the eighteenth-century empirical dictum *esse est percipe* — to be is to be perceived. There is an intriguing circularity about this emergence of a man-centred view of the universe, four centuries after the Copernican revolution broke up the enclosed relationship between man, the cosmos and the creator.

130

Almost as striking as interstellar photography is the way in which certain figures or diagrams have acquired a resonance and authority that is almost that of an icon. The Hertzsprung-Russell diagram, developed between 1908 and 1913, which relates stars' spectral type to luminosity encapsulates some of the basics of astrophysics by showing effectively the life history of stars. The placing of any star on the diagram is like placing one more feature on the map of cosmic space-time. Less technical and equally momentous is the small picture-mosaic constructed to show cosmic background radiation, the echoes of the universe's birth, which has been widely taken as proving the Big Bang theory of cosmology. When this background radiation was first detected, one scientist described it as the 'handwriting of God' on the universe. Perhaps the ultimate cosmological diagrams are those which set out to plot the distribution of galaxies in the universe. The prototype of these shows the familiar, comforting pattern of celestial longitude around its edge, while the galaxies radiate out across 600,000 light years. Like the traditional planisphere, this is a view from above the north celestial pole, but here only a limited latitudinal cross-section is shown. The distinctive pattern at this declination (27–32 degrees) has been christened the 'Stick Man': so we use familiar images to focus and interpret something almost inconceivable, and make it amenable to human thought. These are the new maps of the heavens, and this small diagram is perhaps the most ambitious star chart ever drawn.

The authority accorded to these cosmic images sets up the most compelling echoes of the theme with which this book began — the designation of star-patterns in the ancient near east. Their creators needed landmarks in the sky, as we do. Our sky is no longer their sky, but we still need to elucidate its mysteries by visualizing patterns contained within it. The sun-god, the bull in the heavens, the morning star, all these fed the astral religions of ancient cultures. Today our secular mysticism is sustained by radiant images of galaxies evolving in the vastness of space. Such an image is both an answer to our questions and a further question: it shows how much we know, yet how much remains unexplained. The path towards the unknown is always marked by elements of the known; the map of the heavens is evolving into unexpected forms, but its shaping force has familiar roots deep in the human psyche.

The Polar Stereographic projection

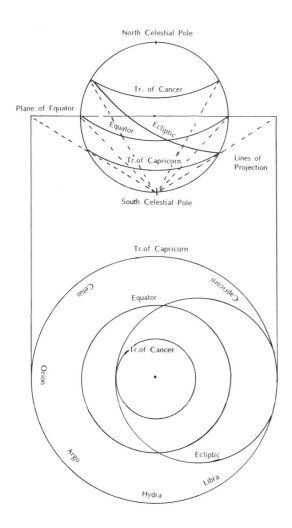

Printed star charts of the northern or southern hemispheres shared the fundamental structure of the astrolabe rete. Neither is a picture of what the human eye sees in the heavens, but is a sophisticated geometric structure, modelled in order to transfer the sphere of heaven on to a two-dimensional plane. The principle is the polar stereographic projection, in which the stars are projected on to the plane of the equator. The point of origin of the projection is the south celestial pole, from which lines are taken to a number of key points on the celestial sphere — the tropics, equator and ecliptic. Points are marked where these lines intersect with the plane of the equator. That plane, viewed from the perpendicular, then becomes a two-dimensional projection of the celestial sphere. The position of all the required stars can be plotted using this method. The result is an ingenious spreading of the entire northern hemisphere, greatly extending what the earthbound observer can see, and extending also what an observer above the north pole of a celestial globe will see. The farther a star lies from the north pole, the farther away it will appear on the plane of projection. In theory the entire heavens might be shown, although the spreading effect would become enormous towards the south pole, indeed the pole itself would become not a point but a circle, forming the boundary of the map. In practice the projection was extended only as far as the Tropic of Capricorn, which formed the edge of the astrolabe. Many printed maps, such as Dürer's, show the ecliptic as the map's border, in which case the point of projection must be the south ecliptic pole. On this projection, the ecliptic becomes an eccentric circle touching both tropics at the solstices, and this is an essential feature of the astrolabe. Because the stereographic projection treats the celestial sphere as a globe, the cycle of the constellations is anti-clockwise, as if seen externally. The theory of the stereographic projection was known to Hipparchus of Rhodes around 150BC, and thereafter to Ptolemy. The earliest surviving post-classical account of it was written in Alexandria in the sixth century AD. In the construction of the astrolabe, the projection was in continuous use by Islamic scholars from the eighth century. In the west, Latin treatises on the astrolabe described it from the eleventh century onwards. This use of geometric principles to create a form of co-ordinate mapping, familiar throughout the middle ages, forms a striking contrast to terrestrial mapping, where such methods were unknown, in western or in Islamic science. It is an open question why celestial maps drawn in this way have not been discovered in any manuscripts, western or oriental, earlier than about 1440, and why it was used only to make the astrolabe rete.

Further Reading

Historical Studies:

K. BRECHER & M. FEIRTAG, eds.: *The Astronomy of the Ancients*, Cambridge, 1979.

O. GINGERICH: *The Great Copernicus Chase*, Cambridge, 1992.

J. B. HARLEY & D. WOODWARD, eds: *History of Cartography*, Vol. 1, Chicago, 1987.

J. B. HARLEY & D. WOODWARD, eds: *History of Cartography*, Vol. 2, Part 1, Chicago, 1992.

D. B. HERMANN: *History of Astronomy from Herschel to Hertzsprung*, English Ed., Cambridge, 1984.

O. NEUGEBAUER: *Astronomy and History*, New York, 1983.

J. D. NORTH: *Fontana History of Astronomy and Cosmology*, London, 1994.

J. D. NORTH: *Stars, Mind and Fate*, London, 1989.

J. D. NORTH: *The Measure of the Universe: a History of Modern Cosmology*, New York, 1990.

J. D. NORTH: *Chaucer's Universe*, Oxford, 1990.

T. S. PATTIE: *Astrology*, London, 1980.

O. PEDERSEN: *Early Physics and Astronomy*, new. ed. Cambridge, 1993.

A. VAN HELDEN: *Measuring the Universe*, Chicago, 1985.

R. S. WESTFALL: *Never at Rest, a biography of Isaac Newton*, Cambridge, 1980.

Illustrated Sources:

B. J. FORD: *Images of Science. A History of Scientific Illustration*, London, 1992.

J. A. LEVENSON: *Circa 1492, Art in the Age of Exploration*, New Haven & London, 1991.

D. MALIN: *A View of the Universe*, Cambridge, 1993.

A. SANDAGE: *The Hubble Atlas of Galaxies*, Washington, 1963.

G. M. SESTI: *The Glorious Constellations*, New York, 1991.

G. S. SNYDER: *Maps of the Heavens*, London, 1984.

A. TURNER: *Early Scientific Instruments, Europe 1400–1800*, London, 1987.

D. WARNER: *The Sky Explored*, Amsterdam, 1979.

Primary Sources:

ARATUS' *Phaenomena*, translated by D. B. Gain, London, 1976.

ARISTOTLE: *Physics* and *On the Heavens*, trans. by R. Hardie, R. Gaye, & J. Stocks, Oxford, 1922.

COPERNICUS: *On the Revolutions of the Heavenly Spheres*, translated by E. Rosen, New York, 1978.

DANTE: *Paradiso: Illuminations to Dante's Divine Comedy*, ed. by J. Pope-Hennessy, London, 1993.

W. DERHAM: *Astro-Theology*, London, 1715 and many subsequent editions.

C. FLAMMARION: *Astronomie populaire*, 1880, English ed. by J. Gore, London, 1895.

O. NEUGEBAUER & R. PARKER: *Egyptian Astronomical Texts*, 4 vols. Providence RI, 1960–69.

PLATO: *Timaeus and Critias*, translated by D. Lee, Harmondsworth, 1965.

PTOLEMY: *Almagest*, English translation by G. J. Toomer, London, 1984.

H. SHAPLEY & H. HOWARTH: *A Source Book in Astronomy*, Cambridge Mass, 1929.